GRASSROOTS DEMOCRACY IN ACTION

About the Authors

Dr. Suresh Misra is currently Associate Professor and Head, Faculty of Public Administration at the Haryana Institute of Public Administration, Gurgaon. He holds his Master's in Political Science from Jawaharlal Nehru University, New Delhi and D.Phil. from Allahabad University.

Dr. Misra had his advance `training in Rural Management at the Development Study Centre, Rehovot, Israel, where he studied the working of the rural cooperatives. He was awarded the prestigious AOTS Scholarship for training in Corporate Governance at AOTS, Tokyo, Japan. He participated in the Training of Trainers (ToT) Programme on Total Quality Management at U.K. Civil Service College, Sunningdale . Recently he attended a ToT programme at Thames Valley University, U.K to refine his training module on Decentralised Planning.

Dr. Misra has authored; Politico-Peasantry Conflict in India (1990), Legislative Framework of Panchayati Raj in India (1993), Popular Participation in Rural Development (1996), and Legislative Status of Panchayati Raj in India (1997). He has edited; *Social Welfare, Poverty Alleviation and New Economic Policy (1995), Environmental Laws in India–Issues and Responses ((1996), Citizen-Friendly Administration (1997) and Humanizing Development – Trends in Public Administration (2001).* He has contributed a number of research papers in professional journals and has also completed a number of research and evaluation studies. He recently prepared a Training Module on Decentralised Planning, sponsored by DOPT and UNDP.

Besides being a Member of a number of professional bodies Dr. Misra was also a member of DRUCC, Northern Railways and TAC, Ministry of Communications, Government of India.

Dr. Rajvir S. Dhaka after his Graduation with Honours in Economics from Delhi University did his Master's in Public Administration and Ph.D from Maharashi Dayanand University, Rohtak. He obtained MBA degree in Human Resource Development from IGNOU, New Delhi. He was awarded UGC Fellowship for doing Ph.D. He is a perceptive researcher, whose interest centers on Public Policy Issues, Rural Development and Good Governance.

Dr. Dhaka has authored : *Participatory Development and Capacity Building (2000)* and co-edited; *Humanizing Development – Trends in Public Administration (2001).* He has contributed a number of research papers in various journals and magazines.

He is currently working as Assistant Professor, Faculty of Public Administration, at Haryana Institute of Public Administration, Gurgaon. He is also associated with Sustainable Development Foundation, New Delhi and presides over SPACE, a NGO based in Haryana. Dr. Dhaka is also a member of a number of professional and academic bodies.

GRASSROOTS DEMOCRACY IN ACTION

(A Study of Working of PRIs in Haryana)

SURESH MISRA

RAJVIR S. DHAKA

CONCEPT PUBLISHING COMPANY, NEW DELHI-110059

The views and opinions expressed in this book are those of the authors and do not necessarily reflect the views of the organizations to which they belong.

ISBN-81-8069-107-1

First Published 2004

Published and Printed by
Ashok Kumar Mittal
Concept Publishing Company
A/15-16, Commercial Block, Mohan Garden,
NEW DELHI-110059 (India)

Phones : 25351460, 25351794
Fax : 0091-11-25357103
E-mail : publishing@conceptpub.com

FOREWORD

In order to revitalize the system of governance from the grassroots, the Panchayati Raj Institutions in the country were constituted as the third tier of authority, with constitutional backing. They have been operational for about a decade now. Their performance in the different States, however, is quite uneven. While, no doubt, a certain degree of empowerment of the marginalised groups in society has been ensured, following the Constitutional amendments and the enabling State legislations, several problems have also surfaced. The new participatory culture of governance at the grassroots does not seem to have taken off in the way it has been envisaged and it has not also fulfilled the expectations of the people. Quite a few studies have appeared in recent years, which have pointed out the various lacunae in the working of the system. At the government level, the reports of the State Finance Commissions have also brought to our notice, the several lags and lapses on the part of both the Panchayats and the State governments. If the various deficiencies that one come across in every State are deemed as 'teething and transition problems', then it is necessary that a 'transition development strategy on an incremental basis' should be devised for each State and implemented rigorously.

Studies and reviews emerging from academics deserve particular attention in this context, as the analysis here will be impartial and constructive in nature, providing clues to some needed correctives and departures in the working of the system. It is in this context that I consider this book, based on an intensive research on the functioning of the Panchayati Raj Institutions in the State of Haryana, as a significant contribution. Although the study is confined to the State of Haryana, its conclusions are bound to have larger and systemic relevance.

The meat of this study is contained in two case studies, one on Panchayat elections, and another on wage employment and rural infrastructure programmes (JRY and JGSY), which contain critical analyses, from which the authors have drawn important lessons. The methodologies used in these case studies are well worth studying for their applicability and replication elsewhere.

The study has brought out that although the Constitutional amendments and follow-up State laws have contributed to the empowerment and representation of the neglected sections of the society, "the quality of local leadership has changed only marginally; and so has the work environment. The State bureaucracy has yet to come to terms with the new dispensation at the local level, and the local leaders have yet to adopt the culture of democratic functioning to win the confidence of the people". The study has rightly observed that new laws in an old socio-economic setting take time to impact the society. The study has also observed that in order to change the working of the PRI's, they have to be further strengthened as legal and Constitutional authorities and also the people who are involved in their working need improvement in themselves. Taking note of the various problems that the PRI's face — lack of participation, bureaucratisation, Pradhan Raj, mal-development in the absence of systematic planning, prevalence of corruption etc. – the authors have discussed the methods to remove the various deficiencies. Some suggestions that they have made, such as selecting one district as a pilot project for planned development in each State, with master plans being drawn for each village, block and district and the application of modern Information Technology to help in the re-development of villages etc. are worth noting.

I congratulate the authors for the excellent work done. I am sure that the book will be a valuable addition to the growing body of Panchayati Raj literature in the country. I also hope that it will be useful to administrators at the State and local levels as well as to students in the universities conducting research on local governance.

K. V. SUNDARAM
Chairman
New Delhi Bhoovigyan Vikas Foundation

PREFACE

People are the means and the end of development but they have different amounts of power and resources and different interest, all of which the state must try to represent and respond to, if it is to act effectively. A state that ignores the needs of a large section of the population in setting and implementing policy is not a capable state. Even with best will and intentions in the world, government is unlikely to meet collective needs efficiently if it does not know what those needs are. Therefore, the need is to revitalise public and democratic institutions and to bring the government closer to the people. This essentially means bringing people's voice into policy making and implementation through greater decentalisation of government power and resources. With the governments unable to meet the growing demands of the people, greater decentralisation of planning and administration offers the chance to match public services more closely with local demands and preference and to build more responsive and accountable government from below.

The working of the Panchayats after the 73rd Amendment Act reveals that the process of decentralisation is more political than administrative. It essentially means sharing political power with local bodies which needs greater political will. Administrative decentalisation without adequate powers, functions and resources is no more a solution to the problems being faced by the Panchayats. In fact it creates vested interests and weakness in the Panchayats. The euphoria generated with the passage of 73rd Amendment Act has now settled down. In most of the states except for cosmetic changes the Panchayats continue to be plagued by various problems. Merely holding elections after every five years and reserving one-third seats in favour of women is not what is expected from Panchayats. It has to lead to greater people's participation in planning, decision-making, sharing the benefits of development and monitoring and evaluation. Since participation requires increased influences and control, it also simultaneously calls for an increased empowerment in economic, social and political terms, which has not taken place yet.

Since long there has been a lack of clarity in regard to the concept of Panchayati Raj itself and the objectives for which it should stand in our political and administrative environment. This continues to exist even after the 73rd Constitutional Amendment Act. "Power to the people appears to be a distant dream." Panchayati Raj has to be viewed as a movement of self-reliance, empowering people and accelerating the pace of rural development. Merely looking at them as administrative or developmental agencies will further aggravate the situation.

The book deals with the on going experimentation with Panchayats in the State of Haryana through case study and relevant data. The study reveals that Constitutional amendments and follow up state laws did make some difference particularly with respect to the representation of the marginalised people. But as far as the working of the institutions is concerned there is much to be desired. The culture of democratic decentralisation is yet to reach the grassroots level.

We have received invaluable help and co-operation from various sources in bringing out this volume. We are thankful to the State Election Commission, Haryana, Directorate of Panchayats, Haryana and various Block Development and Panchayat officers for helping us with relevant data and government instructions. We are thankful to the respondents from various village Panchayats for their co-operation during data collection. Interacting with them was very enriching.

We are grateful to Dr. K.V. Sundaram, welknown international expert on decentralised planning and Chairman, Bhoovigyan Vikas Foundation, New Delhi for writing the foreword and to Prof. R. P. Misra, Former Vice-Chancellor, Allahabad University for his valuable suggestions and guidance. Without his help this book would not have been in the present form.

We will be failing in our duty if we do not thank Ms. Bharti Misra, Deep Public School, New Delhi, for reading the manuscripts and give useful suggestions and Dr. Sunita Dhaka, Lecturer, Public Administration, Govt. College, Gurgaon and Ms. Manisha for her tireless efforts in compiling and tabulating data.

Finally we are thankful to Sri Ashok Kumar Mittal, Concept Publishing Company for publishing this volume .

Gurgaon
1 January, 2004

SURESH MISRA
RAJVIR S. DHAKA

CONTENTS

Foreword *v*
Preface *vii*

1. **Introduction** 1
   Evolution of Pachayati Raj in India *6*
      Pre-Independence Development *6*
   Post-Independence Changes *10*
      Balwantrai Mehta Committee *11*
      Ashok Mehta Committee *12*
      Rajiv Gandhi's Initiative *13*
      73rd Constitutional Amendment Act *15*
      Gram Sabha : The Fulcrum of the PRIs *16*
      Haryana Falls in Line *21*
   Concluding Remarks *24*

2. **Panchayati Raj in Haryana** 26
   Historical Roots *26*
   Post-Independence Developments *27*
   Panchayati Raj in the New State of Haryana *28*
   Haryana Panchayati Raj Act, 1994 *30*
      Gram Sabha *30*
      Gram Panchayats *31*
      Panchayat Samiti *35*
      Zila Parishad *40*

   Panchayati Raj System: A Critique *44*
      Gram Vikas Samiti *48*
      Financial Resources *50*
      Internal Checks *51*
         Zila Parishad, Panipat *52*
         Panchayat Samiti, Sadhera *52*
         Panchayat Samiti, Nahar, *53*
         Panchayat Samiti, Bahadurgarh *53*
         Panchayat Samiti, Barwala *53*

Panchayat Samiti, Mandi Dhabwali *53*
Panchayat Samiti, Rania *53*
Ex. Engineer, Panchayat Raj (HRDF), Hissar *54*
Ex. Engneer. PR (HRDF), Sirsa *54*
Ex. Engineer, (HRDF), Thaneswar *54*
Panchayat Samiti (HRDF), Rajound *54*
Panchayat Samiti, Ellenabad *54*
Analysis of the Situation *55*

3. Changing Electoral Processes 69
Panchayati Raj Elections *70*
Electoral Politics *71*
Some Chronic Problems *73*
Impact of Constitutional Amendment *74*
Appointment of State Election Commission *74*
Registration of Voters *75*
Qualification of Contestants *77*
Reservation for Weaker Sections *79*
Electoral Rules *80*
Conduct of Elections *81*
Arrangement for Elections *82*
Delimitation of Electoral Wards *83*
Nomination and Scrutiny *83*
Allotment of Election Symbols *85*
Symbols Designs and Size of Ballot Papers *87*
Counting of Votes *88*
Declaration of Results *89*
Election Petitions *90*
Role of Government Officers *91*

4. Panchayat Elections – 2000 94
Conduct of Elections *94*
Limit on Expenditure *97*
Videography of Elections *99*
Restrictions on Use of Vehicles *100*
Unanimous Elections *102*
Violence in Elections *104*

5. Emerging Leadership 108
Methodology of the Study *110*
Gram Panchayats *111*
Socio-economic Profile of Elected Members GPs *111*
Socio-economic Profile of Sarpanches (General) *116*
Socio-economic Profile of Women Sarpanches *119*
Socio-economic Profile of Members of the PSs and ZPs *122*

6. Panchayats at Work : A Case Study of JRY 131
Methodology *133*
Social Profile of the Respondents *135*
Age, Sex and Caste *135*
Education and Occupation *136*
Previous Experience *138*
Knowledge about JRY *138*
Peripheral Role of Gram Sabha *139*
Availability and Utilisation of Funds *140*
Involvement of Contractors *141*
Durability of Assets *143*
Perception of the JRY Beneficiaries *144*
Consumption Pattern of JRY Beneficiaries *146*
Jawahar Gram Samridhi Yojana (JGSY) *149*

7. Panchayati Raj Institutions : The Reforms They Must Undergo 158
Major Problems *159*
Lack of Participation *159*
Bureaucratisation *160*
Pradhan Raj *161*
Maldevelopment *161*
Corruption *162*
How to bring PRIs Back on the Rails *163*
Another Bout of Constitutional Amendment *163*
Primacy of Gram Sabha *163*
Secure Funding *164*
Ensuring Meaningful Development *165*

Master Planning *165*
Application of Information Technology *166*
Classification of Villages *167*
Recapturing Gandhi's Vision of PRIs *168*

Bibliography 169
Index 175

1

INTRODUCTION

Almost three-fourths of people of India live in rural areas, which comprise of half a million villages. This amounts to over 750 million people, more than the combined population of all the developed countries of the world minus Japan and South Korea. Over and above this huge number, there are at least 100 million urban peasants – the rural poor who have migrated to cities in the last few decades to seek better opportunities. They are informal sector workers struggling hard to make their two ends meet. They live in slums and squatter settlements of India's large cities. That makes a total of 850 million people. Gandhi's view that 'India lives in villages' still holds good. Development in India can be meaningful only if people living in these villages become its beneficiaries.

The importance of the rural sector in the Indian economy has not changed much during the last fifty years or so even if the contribution that agriculture, the main productive base of rural India, makes to the national GDP secularly declined during the last three decades or so; currently it is less than 30 per cent of the total. The service sector accounts for 41 per cent and the industrial sector for 29 per cent. The other parameters have, however, remained unchanged. Agriculture still employs about two-thirds of the labour force and the overall dependence of the people on agriculture is still very high; almost 70 per cent. Agriculture ensures food and fibre supply, it provides skilled as well unskilled manpower to other sectors of the economy, and makes unmatched contribution to ecological and environmental security.

During the last five decades a number of policies, programmes and projects were launched to revive and strengthen India's rural economy and polity. The rural areas are now far different from what they were prior to the independence of the country in 1947. But the structure of the rural economy and society has not yet changed substantially enough to harness all the natural and human potentials and to generate development from within. Rural economy continues to be an agricultural economy in the grip of age-old poverty syndrome. Rural society is highly fractured and fragmented and the village solidarity that once was its hallmark is no longer there. Environmentally too, village India is in distress. Pollution of land, water and air is no longer a problem of large cities. Rural areas too are adversely affected by this menace.

Why has rural India lagged behind? It is not the place to go into this question in detail but a few observations will not be out of place. The factors, which have made the situation as it is, are: bureaucratic administration, weak local institutions, distorted concept of development, pro-urban policies, and lack of integrated approach. India has adopted the western model of development wherein development is equated with economic growth. The people are treated as instruments of development, not the very objects of development. It was presumed that higher national income was all that was needed; that higher national income without a sound distributive policy would amount to neglect of the weaker sections of the society; and that man does not live by bread alone was almost forgotten. Related to this misconception about development was the pro-urban development policy. Developed countries being highly urbanised and industrialised, urbanisation and industrialisation were treated as two sides of the same coin. Industrialisation was considered essential for economic growth. Since cities had the necessary infrastructure for industrial development, they were accorded priority over villages. Whatever resources were earmarked for rural areas went to agriculture. The other sectors of the rural life, particularly the social sector, were not accorded the importance they deserved. Only those who had access to agricultural resources benefited from rural development efforts. The landless and marginal farmers benefited least.

It is now clear that all the three premises were misconceived. Development essentially means human development-transformation of life in its varied manifestations. It is the people who are the objects as well as the subjects of development. By people we mean all the people, rich or poor, educated or illiterate, urbanites or ruralites, men or women, young or old. Economic development involving improvements in income, assets, production, consumption etc. constitute only one, even if very important, aspect of life. It does not represent the whole life.

Over emphasis on economic development, neglecting other aspects of human life, is neither possible nor desirable. Within the economic sector, the sub-sectors like industry, agriculture, and services constitute inseparable parts of a single integrated system of economy. Similarly, the urban and rural settlements do not stand apart; they are interdependent. One sector cannot be developed at the cost of other sectors. Development process follows Liebig's Law: Overdose of one factor does not produce optimum results. It often proves counterproductive. As such the over emphasis on economic aspects of life at the cost of culture, society, polity and ecology can produce a highly explosive situation.

The past policies have focussed on urban industrial development. People were treated as the means of development, not the ends of development. The ends constituted increased GDP, per capita income, agricultural and industrial production, and improvements in technology and infrastructure. People became human resources to be used for development in the same way as natural resources are used. Recognition of man as the object as well as subject of development shifts the focus from the economy to human personality. What type of man emerges from the development process in vogue becomes the real test of success or failure of development. In this context the development indicators we use today give us only a partial picture of development.

Given the situation as it is, the question is how to alter it so that rural development is accelerated? It is now a well accepted fact that development is multi-faceted; it covers all aspects of human life; and it cannot be given or imposed from above. Unless the people who are the very subject and object of development are prepared to initiate development, to participate in it fully and to take responsibility for it, it cannot be achieved in true sense. It is quite another thing that a few physical facilities and assets are created by outside agencies but in the long-run even these facilities will prove dead investments. Real development means human development and human development needs a far different mindset and approach than what prevails today.

There is no formal school to train people in their own development. The training ground is environment in which they live and work. Development includes understanding of the environment, its potentials and their own abilities, needs and requirements apart from using the environment to meet their own goals and objectives. Let them engage themselves in what they consider to be good for them and learn from the mistakes they commit. This means freedom to act and self-governance which Mahatma Gandhi called *Swaraj*. In the context of rural India, it means *Gram Swaraj* which in the modern context boils down to grassroots democracy.

A state that ignores the needs of a large section of the population in setting and implementing development policies cannot be said to be a democratic and forward looking state. Even with the best will and intentions, governments often fail to respond to the collective needs and aspirations of the people. It is more so with governments which are highly centralised, bureaucratised and control oriented. They prefer to do things for the people rather than encouraging people to do things for themselves, manage their own affairs and become self-reliant. There is no way of changing this character and culture except by democratising them and bringing them closer to the people. That means direct control of people over the government machinery and bringing their voice into policy making and planning. This implies decentralisation of power of decision-making and resource allocation from centralised authorities to the grassroots level.

The framers of Indian Constitution were aware of the bureaucratic functioning of the governmental machinery. They therefore envisaged a decentralised democratic system of governance and direct participation of the people in decision-making down to the grassroots level through periodic elections to national parliament, state legislatures, city municipalities and Village Panchayats. The institutions created for the purpose however did not come to the expectations. Below the state legislatures, institutional development remained stunted. The elected bodies were there but only in name. They had no powers and resources to do anything worthwhile.

Evidence from a mixed bag of development projects supports the contention that top-down approaches may be more efficient in offering palliative remedies but they rarely, if ever at all, cure the disease. Experiments with participatory approaches have convinced both national and international agencies of the merits of community involvement in the conceptualisation, planning and execution of all local level development projects.

Community participation is beneficial in many ways. It brings disparate people together for joint and co-operative efforts; it trains people in solving their own problems; it ensures fullest utilisation of local talent, local resources and local level environmental sustainability. The enhanced quality of life felt by the participants of such projects is an additional advantage. The external agencies, institutions and interest groups can play important roles in community development but not much can be achieved unless the people themselves directly or through their representatives are involved in it. Schemes, which have been implemented by governments bypassing the people and their leaders have run into trouble. One can see a large number of foundation stones, hand pumps, irrigation channels, roads, school buildings and what not littered around and in ruins in rural parts of India. They have been executed by the governmental agencies ostensibly to help the people enjoy a better quality of life. The budgeted resources have been utilised, but the projects have failed. People have no use for most of them. Local leaders form the bridge between official agencies and the people.

A well-known paradox in community development is the frequent need for an outside "triggering" agent to initiate action. It may be a NGO, higher level government authorities, or business and industry or even international agency. This intervention works if from the very beginning there exists a clear commitment to enlist and sustain people's direct participation at every step of project planning and execution. Development strategies can become meaningful only if the people consider them right and if they have control over their implementation at every step on the way. People act through their own institutions and their own representative elected through a democratic process. In rural India Panchayati Raj Institutions are designed to represent the people and their voice.

Evolution of Panchayati Raj in India

Panchayati Raj in India is as old as Indian civilisation. Its history goes back to the Vedic times and according to some even pre-Vedic times. To understand Indian polity and Indian culture one has to understand the nature and functions of Village Panchyats. Like the joint family system, Village Panchayats survived all ups and downs until the British take over of India in the nineteenth century. Even during the British era they continued to function informally and saved the Indian society from disintegration. After gaining independence, one of the priority concerns of the new government was to revive the Village Panchayats. But in the midst of the ideological confusion that prevailed at that time and the insurmountable problems emerging from the partition of the country, not much could be done. And when the time to do something came, the thinking as well as the priorities of the government had changed.

Now there is a renewed effort to put the Panchayati Raj System on the rails again. In this chapter, we propose to deliberate on the reasons for the renewed interest in this age-old system of governance at the grassroots level and the problems and prospects that lie ahead.

Pre-Independence Development

The old Village Panchayats in India which Sir Charles Metcalfe described as little village republics were not based on legislative enactments but were custom-based and tradition bound institutions sustained by a reciprocity of interests between land-owners bound together by ties of kinship and principles and pre-emption on one hand and the farm labourers and tillers of the soil on the other. It was a status governed static arrangement where mobility hardly existed. There was a prevailing sense of an equity based consensus of local opinion but no contract based rules of law, the foundation of modern democracy. The land legislation enacted under British rule was in recognition of this principle of contract which tended to free individuals from the exercise of communal delegations and rendering them subject to law which recognised the right to property in their individual capacity. The rule of law encouraged individualism and increased litigation, which, in effect, sapped the foundations of the old village communities.

In the early stages of British rule it was the logic of events and of necessity which was mainly responsible for cropping up a system of local administration. The demand for democratic decentralisation came from the educated elite who wanted share in the exercise of power and patronage. It was limited to local bodies and municipalities and based on the principle that local needs must be met by local taxation. This principle was incorporated by Lord Mayo in a decentralisation scheme formulated by the Government in 1870 which made provision for local funds being raised locally by municipal and rural boards to meet their local requirements.

The main object of Lord Mayo's scheme was to relieve the imperial finances of the management of local needs. Lord Ripon extended a decentralised system of finance by transferring from the "provincial" to local activity such additional items of receipts and charges as might equalise local and municipal taxation to secure uniform progress in their development throughout the country. He not only carried out but also developed the policy of his predecessors.

The first period for our analysis embarks with the announcement of the Government of India Resolution on local self-government in 1882. Hitherto local government had remained almost wholly non-Indian and, therefore, from Indian point of view, was to a great extent neither local nor self-government.

Lord Ripon's reforms constitute a landmark in the history of local self-government in India, for they attempted to put it for the first time on a popular elective basis. The nominated district committees then existed had not proved a success. "Experience proves", says Ripon's Resolution of 1882, "that district committees are as a rule very badly attended by members not actually residing in the vicinity of headquarters stations. Those who do attend have frequently no intimate acquaintance with the needs of outlying parts of the district. The consequences is that undue attention is given to the requirements of the immediate neighbourhood of the central stations or that the business falls entirely into the hands of the district officer.

Lord Ripon's Resolution

Lord Ripon's first scheme was elaborated in his Resolution of September 30, 1880, on financial decentralisation. It said that though considerable progress in the direction of local self-government had been made since the days of Lord Mayo, when the subject was first taken up. It was very unequal in the different provinces and that the time had now come for further practical developments. With this end in view it invited the provincial governments to scrutinise carefully the provincial and local accounts. Lord Ripon was not satisfied with the proposals submitted by the provincial governments for the reform of local self-government specially in the rural areas. It appeared to him that his ideas on the subject had not been fully understood. Accordingly, he proceeded to explain somewhat more fully than he had hitherto done, the general mode in which he would wish to see effect given to the principle of local self-government throughout British India outside the Presidency towns.

In May 18, 1882 came Lord Ripon's famous Resolution. It has been regarded as the Magna Carta of local self-government in India. The Resolution's emphasis was mainly on the political and popular training of educated Indians through these local representative institutions. For the resolution categorically stated that the measure was "chiefly designed as an instrument of political and popular education" of the 'rapidly growing' class of 'intelligent' and 'public-spirited men' who it considered to be 'bad policy' and sheer waste of power to ignore or not to utilise.

The Resolution recommended that the smallest administrative unit the sub-division, taluka or the tehsil shall ordinarily be placed under a local board. Above the local boards the provincial governments might create district boards, with powers of co-ordination or control. The local boards to be constituted so as to have on them a preponderant non-official majority, ordinarily not less than two-third of their entire membership. The term of the members was to be two years and compulsory retirement by rotation was to be provided for.

Regarding finance, the Resolution repeated the principles laid down earlier and pleaded for the widest budgetary freedom to the local bodies. It further said that in case of grave abuse of power or neglect of duty, the Central Government should have the power to supersede the local boards. Lord Ripon felt, that there would be a need for the collector to remain the chairman or even a member of the local bodies.

The next important development relates to the Royal Commission on Decentralisation (1909). After reviewing the working of the local and the district boards in the various provinces of the British India, the Commission came to the conclusion that due chiefly to their unrepresentative character and inadequate powers these bodies had not been a success, "the want of success of the existing system", said the report, seem to us to be mainly due to two reasons; firstly, that the boards have hitherto not possessed real power; secondly, that the methods of election adopted have not generally speaking provided for due representation. To remove the defects, it recommended the creation of a genuine electoral consisting of the members of the Village Panchayats, the provision for an elective majority on all boards, and a due representation to minorities through nominations.

These recommendations received the attention of Government of India in its resolution on local self-government of 1915. In 1918, the Montague-Chelmsford Report was published. It contained the proposals for immediate political advance, a new significance came to be attached to the question of local self-government. The report further said that responsible institutions will not be stably rooted until they become broad-based, and far sighted Indian politicians will find no field in which their energies can be more profitably thrown than in developing the boroughs and the communes of their country. These proposals were untimely embodied in Government of India's Resolution of 1918. It accepted fully and frankly the principle of substantial elective majorities of all the boards.

Some of the popular governments which assumed office under the Act of 1919 tried to bring about a radical renovation of the form and structure of rural local self-government. But the results were disappointing especially from the point of view of later day analysts who have evaluated the evolution of local government in terms of local autonomy. It has been observed that the Panchayats established under the Act of 1920 were merely a pale shadow of the glorious institutions that flourished in the villages in the earliest times. They were not fully representative, their powers were limited and their finances were meagre and fluctuating and there was no provision for regular and substantial aid from government. The view is that the formation of popular governments under Dyarchy virtually represented the last opportunity for strengthening local bodies in the pre-Independence era. The next opportunity offered by the Government of India Act, 1935 was too short-lived. Thus, it can be said that these bodies in pre-Independence India were shacked with an extensive network of supervision and control and catered to the needs of the imperialist power and as seen local self-government did not emerge as true centres of power and suffered from a number of weaknesses.

Post-Independence Changes

Any discussion on Panchayati Raj Institutions and their role in local level development would be incomplete without referring to the contributions of two committees, one headed by Balwantrai Mehta and the other by Ashok Mehta both very eminent political figures devoted to rural development. The reports of these committees have been discussed in many forum and publication yet their relevance continues undiminished partly because they laid the foundation of Panchayati Raj Institutions in India in post-Independence era and partly because they emanated from a deep commitment and foresight of the contemporary political leadership towards Panchayati Raj Institutions.

Balwantrai Mehta Committee

A study team under the leadership of Balwantrai Mehta was set up in 1957 to review the working of the Community Development Programme and National Extension Service. Among other things, it recommended the setting up of a three-tier Panchayati Raj System at the village, block and district levels to ensure participatory rural development. The Panchayat at the village level, the Panchayat Samiti at the block level and the Zila Parishad at the district level were organically linked through the device of indirect elections. It suggested a new administrative structure specially trained to work with people and promote development from below.

The committee made a distinction between delegation of power and devolution of power. The latter amounted to decentralisation whereby the government divests itself completely of certain duties and responsibilities and devolves them to local level bodies. Delegation on the other hands means engaging the local governments as agents of the higher level governments to accomplish certain tasks. The final authority rests with the higher level governments. Devolution was thus seen as an orderly transfer of authority, resources and institutional capabilities to local governments. Democratic decentralisation, to become a reality, must be backed by a political will. Following the recommendations of the Balwantrai Mehta Committee, Panchayati Raj legislation was introduced in various States starting with Rajasthan and followed by Bihar, Gujarat, Punjab, Maharashtra and Uttar Pradesh in 1961; Madhya Pradesh in 1962; West Bengal in 1963; and Himachal Pradesh in 1968. Though Jammu and Kashmir, Kerala, Manipur and Tripura had also introduced legislations but, these States had only one tier (at the lowest level) and, therefore, in a strict sense they did not follow the Panchayati Raj concept as envisaged in the report.

Based on the provisions in the State legislations, it is possible to classify the states into three categories. In the first category, the recommendations of the Balwantrai Mehta

Committee were fully incorporated. Members of the Gram Panchayat were directly elected by village adults; they in turn elected the members of the Panchayat Samiti at the Block level and the members of the Zila Parishad at the district level were elected by the members of the respective lower tiers. In the second category (characterised by the Maharashtra pattern) though there was a three-tier system, it was not closely knit as in the first category. The members of the Gram Panchayat and Zila Parishad were directly elected by village adults. There were also some differences in the functions too. The third category followed an intermediary pattern between the Balwantrai Mehta model and Maharashtra model. In certain States, the district level body was either non-existent or weak; for all practical purposes only two-tiers existed.

The initial enthusiasm of setting up Panchayati Raj Institutions along the lines of Balwantrai Mehta Committee report was short lived. A number of programmes introduced in the sixties for agricultural and rural development created various parallel agencies at the village level. In most cases the Panchayati Raj Institutions were not associated with these activities. Thus, the period of the late sixties and the seventies witnessed a somewhat inactive period for Panchayati Raj Institutions.

Ashok Mehta Committee

Concerned about the lamentable state of the Panchayat Raj Institutions, another committee under the chairmanship of Ashok Mehta was appointed in 1977 to review the working of the Panchayati Raj Institutions. It recommended a two-tier system, with the district as the point of decentralisation below the State level. It considered Block to be too large an area to ensure people's participation and village to be too small to be a viable unit for planning and development. Hence it suggested that a group of ten villages should form a Mandal and the Mandal should have an elected body. Thus it introduced Mandal Panchayats between the erstwhile district and Block Panchayats. It felt that Mandal Panchayats could handle the development tasks better. The Committee recognised the existence of other tiers (such as Block, Taluk) in various States, but wanted these tiers to be gradually replaced by the two-tier system.

The Ashok Mehta Committee's recommendations made the prevailing confusion more confounded. Instead of revitalising the three-tier system, which had come to stay, it recommended the dismantling of it. The States found it convenient to choose their pet patterns. Some of the States continued with the old system, some adopted a mixed pattern taking something from Balwantrai Mehta Report and something from Ashok Mehta Report. Many of them did nothing and allowed the Panchayati Raj System to degenerate. Elections to these bodies did not take place in time and some of the States did not hold elections for decades and kept the Panchayati Raj Institutions under perpetual supersession. Even where elections were held, the representation of the weaker sections like the Scheduled Castes, Scheduled Tribes and women was inadequate. The Panchayats did not get enough powers and resources from the States to carry out their responsibilities.

Thus the Panchayati Raj Institutions could not acquire the status and dignity of viable and responsive local self-governing bodies. Soon the very concept of Panchayati Raj became blurred and the objectives for which it was created were forgotten. Political factionalism rendered developmental thrusts they were designed to possess either warped or diluted. Corruption, inefficiency, scant regard for procedures, political interference in day-to-day administration, parochial loyalties, motivated actions etc. seriously marred their utility for the average villager.

Rajiv Gandhi's Initiative

Committed to the progress of India at an accelerated speed, Rajiv Gandhi proposed a number of economic, social and political reforms. One of them was the revival of the Panchayati Raj Institutions. He was convinced that rural India would not progress unless grassroots democracy became a reality. He was also convinced that given the then Constitutional dispensation with respect to the Panchayati Raj, there was no way of reviving them. He, therefore, mooted the idea of amending the Constitution to confer on institutions like Panchayats in villages and municipal governments in cities Constitutionally guaranteed executive as well as financial powers and responsibilities to manage their affairs. The underlying thesis behind the idea was that unless these institutions are given Constitutional authority, the State governments would not allow them to grow.

Any change in the Constitution to transfer certain powers from the States to the local institutions meant certain curtailment of power of the State governments. Only a strong Central government could initiate this action. When Shri Rajiv Gandhi became Prime Minister of India after the assassination of Mrs. Indira Gandhi in 1984, he had behind him a wide support of the people from all over the country. He wanted to take India on a faster track to the twenty-first century. The revitalisation of the Panchayati Raj Institutions through Constitutional amendment was one of his top priorities.

The idea behind the amendment was to confer Constitutional status to the local bodies so that interference by the State governments in matters earmarked for local self-government was minimal. It widened the scope for people's participation by enhancing and ensuring adequate representation of women, poor and deprived sections of the society in all elected bodies. Mechanisms for the decentralisation of administration and development works down to the village, block and district levels were created. Powers were vested in elected representatives enabling them to determine the needs and priorities, to initiate socio-economic development and to build a society based on democratic principles. The people were given an opportunity to enhance their capability and capacity to plan and execute development programmes, projects and schemes from below.

For democracy to be successful the grassroots organisations have to be strong and the local authorities have to respond to the felt needs of the people. The citizens have to have faith in the efficacy and efficiency of the administrative system so that the distance between people and the government is reduced. The instruments of good governance have to be accessible to all rich or poor, literate or illiterate, men or women. It is here that local governments can play a crucial role in strengthening democracy and bringing about a responsive, accountable, effective and people friendly administration at the local level.

73rd Constitutional Amendment Act

Constitutional changes to empower the Panchayati Raj Institutions ware carried out through 73rd Constitutional Amendment Act, 1992 which was passed by the Parliament and came into operation with effect from April 25, 1993. As stated earlier it conferred Constitutional status to Panchayati Raj Institutions and accorded them durability, continuity, and financial viability. Provisions were made for due representation of weaker sections of the society, and regular and periodic elections. Since then the government became a three tiers system – centre, state, and local, instead of only two tier system *i.e.* Centre and State.

The Act provided for activation of the institution of Gram Sabha, establishment of Village Panchayats, intermediate tier between Village Panchayat and Zila Panchayat. It was left to the discretion of the States to determine the area of the intermediate level depending upon the local conditions. Some States may be too small to have intermediate level. Some special provisions were made for some of the States. Seats were reserved for Scheduled Castes and Scheduled Tribes at each level in proportion to their population, and for women to the tune of 33 per cent for all positions. It also provided for a clear term of five years for every elected body and in case a Panchayat was dissolved due to some reasons then the elections to constitute the new Panchayat had to be held within six months of such dissolution. It provided for the constitution of State level commissions to conduct elections and to devolve necessary financial resources to these bodies. Besides authorising the Panchayats to levy, collect and appropriate local taxes, it also provided for making grants-in-aid to the Panchayats from the consolidated fund of the State. As per the provisions of the newly introduced Schedule XI of the Constitution, the Panchayats were empowered to prepare and implement development programmes and schemes with respect to 29 subjects.

The salient features of the 73rd Constitutional Amendment Act are summarised below :

1. After Part VIII of the Constitution a separate Part IX has been added to the Constitution with the addition in

Article 243 A to 243 D and a fresh schedule called the Eleventh Schedule, enumerating the powers and functions of Panchayati Raj Institutions, has been incorporated.

2. The Gram Sabha has found its legitimate place in the Act and a three-tier model of Panchayati Raj except for the States having less than twenty lakh population has been adopted.
3. There is provision for one-third reservation of seats for Scheduled Castes/Tribes and a similar number of seats for women including the Scheduled Castes/Tribes women. Even the office of the chairperson is reserved for Scheduled Castes/Tribes and women.
4. The term of office for all categories of Panchayati Raj representatives has been fixed for five years and if such bodies are dissolved within the five-year period, fresh elections for the remainder of the period will take place within six months from the date of its dissolution.
5. In regard to powers and functions of Panchayati Raj bodies, the Act says that apart from the functions listed in the Eleventh Schedule, the State Legislature, may assign the preparation of plans for economic development and social justice and their implementation to Panchayati Raj Institutions. For the audit of Panchayati Raj accounts the Act says that the State machinery will audit their accounts too.
6. The Act also provides for constituting a finance commission for each State to look after the financial position of the Panchayati Raj Institutions. Article 280 of the Constitution has been appropriately amended for this purpose. Similarly, in regard to elections, the Act makes it the responsibility of the State Election Commission.

Gram Sabha : The Fulcrum of the PRIs

To give effective and efficient services, an organisation must have a functional structure that operates democratically and maintains a productive flow of information both vertically and horizontally to keep track of the unwanted deviations from policy norms. And it is the Gram Sabha in Panchayati Raj System that has been assigned this role of monitoring and evaluation apart from prioritising needs and earmarking resources for specific projects at the village level. It is the most representative institution of democratic decision-making at the village level. The accountability of the elected representatives of the Panchayats to the electorate is ensured through the Gram Sabha. Panchayats as the basic unit of self-government is expected to bridge the gap between the people and the government and to ensure that development takes place as per needs, wishes and priorities of the people. It provides an organic link between various tiers of government. The success of the village government depends almost entirely on how the Gram Sabhas function.

In the new dispensation, the Gram Sabha has become a Constitutional reality vested with certain powers and functions. Its composition ensures the participation of all the adult residents of the village. It has the power to discuss and review all development problems/programmes of the village, select beneficiaries for various programmes, plan for local improvements including the provision of minimum needs and the welfare of the weaker sections.

The Gram Sabha is charged with the responsibility of ensuring participatory management of development programmes within its jurisdiction. It is expected that this body will be much more democratic and accountable to the citizens; it will maintain transparency in decision-making and resource allocation. The system of Panchayati Raj will achieve its desired objectives only if the Gram Sabha is able to discharge its obligations well.

One of the major reasons for the failure of Panchayati Raj System to take roots in our country in the past has been the inability of the Gram Sabha to discharge its responsibilities. The Constitutional Amendment has not changed the situation materially. Both Constitutionally and legally, the Panchayat edifice is built on a strong foundations of the Gram Sabha, yet it remains the weakest link in the system. Gram Sabhas have not been able to cope with the new social realities. It is still a victim of the prevailing rural power structure, which favours the *status quo*. In a number of States, Gram Sabhas rarely, if ever, meet; the Gram Pradhan and Panchayat secretary jointly draft the resolutions on behalf of the Sabha. Since most of the Pradhans are not very knowledgeable and many are even illiterate, the local officials manipulate the whole system often to their advantage. The nexus between the officials and the elected representatives all the way from Gram Pradhan to Zila Parishad chairman further weakens the Gram Sabhas. In spite of the Gram Sabhas being given wide powers under the 73rd Amendment and subsequent amendments in the State laws, barring a few States, they continue to remain dormant. The reservation of seats for the women and the other deprived sections of the society has not so far improved their participation and role.

To make the Gram Sabhas more vibrant, a sub-group of the Task Force on Panchayati Raj constituted by the Union Ministry of Rural Development in its report submitted in 1999 recommended among others :

1. Appointment of specified government officials or officers of intermediate/Zila Panchayats as observers for Gram Sabha meetings. It would be helpful in proper reporting of the proceedings and follow-up of the decisions taken.
2. Holding of Gram Sabha meetings throughout the country under a mobilisation, movement called "Gram Sabha Abhiyana" spread over a period of two weeks. This would be the most practical way of ensuring the regularity of Gram Sabha meetings.
3. The agenda of the Gram Sabha should be so chalked out that they should be of interest to the bulk of its membership and must cover a range of subjects that vitally affect their day-to-day life like the management and functioning of village schools, village water supply schemes, health centre, *Anganwadi,* and maintenance of records etc.
4. The Gram Sabha should not act merely as a recommendatory body or a debating forum of the people. The views expressed and decisions taken in the Gram Sabhas should be respected by the Gram

Panchayats as well higher level Panchayats. Grievances of the people should be redressed with speed and sincerity and their legitimate demands should be met without delay.

5. If the decisions of the Gram Sabha cannot be implemented, the Gram Panchayats should give the reasons for non-compliance to Gram Sabhas.

If these measures are adopted in their true spirits, Gram Sabha can become a vibrant institution and the pace of development in rural areas will also be accelerated. Recognising the potential role of Gram Sabha in strengthening participatory democracy and decentralised planning and also in recognition of the past neglect of the Gram Sabhas, the Government of India declared 1999-2000 as the Year of the Gram Sabha.

Since the introduction of Panchayati Raj System in India in a formal sense, the problem of non-participation of the people in Gram Sabha meetings has been a major weakness. It has been noted by policy-makers, planners, academicians and the governmental agencies. A number of efforts were made from time-to-time to overcome this problem. Recently the Ministry of Rural Development, Government of India, requested the State governments to consider a package of changes during the "Year of Gram Sabha" to improve the situation. The package included:

1. The relationship between the Gram Sabha and the Gram Panchayat may be the same as between the legislature and the government. The Panchayat should be accountable to Gram Sabha in unequivocal terms. The members of the Panchayat should hold office only so long as they enjoy the confidence of Gram Sabha.
2. The Gram Sabha should have full powers for determining the priorities for various programmes in the village and approval of the budget. Prior approval of the Gram Sabhas should be made mandatory for taking up any programme in the village. Certification of expenditure and propriety in financial dealings should be made mandatory and Gram Sabha is responsible for that.

3. The management of natural resources including land, water and forest by any authority whatsoever should be made subject to the concurrence of the Gram Sabha. Consultation with the Gram Sabha should be mandatory before acquisition of land for public purpose and other forms of land transfer.
4. The Gram Sabha should be vested with full authority to manage all affairs concerning intoxicants including their manufacture, sale, transport and consumption and also enforcement of total prohibition, if the Gram Sabha so desires.
5. Participation of women, SC/ST members in the Gram Sabha should be made mandatory with suitable provisions for their presence in the quorum for Gram Sabha meetings.
6. The Gram Sabha should have the power to evolve its own procedure for conducting its business including decision making following the principles of natural justice, etc.

The State governments have been advised to ensure that the Gram Sabhas meet frequently and regularly and that at least one meeting is held in each quarter of the year preferably on a day of national holiday. The whole objective is to make Gram Sabha an effective instrument of planning and development at the local level.

The suggestions listed above if implemented would make radical change in the functioning of the PRIs in India. But not much has happened and business of Panchayats and its various organs continues to be as usual. Most of the Gram Sabha members do not identify themselves with these bodies; a sizeable number of them do not even know that there is anything like Gram Sabha. And, therefore, the question of their participation in it does not arise. To day's village is not a homogeneous entity; it is a highly fractured and heterogeneous entity. The solidarity that once was the hallmark of Indian village is almost lost. The Panchayat elections in the past might have not done much good to the village but they have surely succeeded in making them outward looking and highly divided. The community life based on mutual help, care and self respect even if within the pernicious system of castes has now given way to individualism. If the Gram Sabhas and other village institutions do not function according to the letter and spirit of the law, it is because of the perversion of the democratic values enshrined in Indian Constitution and the debasement of the political system that runs the democratic institutions.

Haryana Falls in Line

When Punjab was bifurcated in 1966 and Haryana became a separate State, even though Panchayati Raj System existed, it had not taken deep roots. These institutions did not enjoy much autonomy due to State Government's control over them. The Panchayats in the State continued to be governed by the Punjab Gram Panchayat Act of 1952 and the Punjab Panchayat Samitis and Zila Parishad Act of 1961. The State had a three-tier Panchayat system at the village, intermediate and the district level. However in 1972, the Zila Parishads were abolished. Due to the abolition of the Zila Parishad, the structural and institutional aspects of Panchayats had become weak. As a result the organic link between the Village Panchayat and the Block Panchayat with that of the district was missing.

In due course of time the administrative and political apparatus came to dominate these bodies. This resulted in a gradual erosion of the authority and powers of the Panchayats thereby undermining the position of the elected representatives. The role of development administration was devalued by tightening of the grip on these bodies by the local elites, bureaucracy and the political leadership. Due to these factors the very objective of democratic decentralisation was defeated and the Panchayats in the State remained dormant till the enactment of the 73rd Constitutional Amendment Act.

Keeping in view the 73rd Constitutional Amendment Act, the Panchayats in the State were revitalised under the Haryana Panchayati Raj Act of 1994. The Act envisages a three-tier Panchayat system in the State with a fixed tenure of five years. Seats have been reserved in favour of Scheduled Castes and women. It also provides for the constitution of a Finance Commission and an Election Commission. For the first time under the new Act, the Panchayats in the State were constituted in 1995. At present there are 6,019 Panchayats, 114 Panchayat Samitis, and 19 Zila Parishads with a total electorate of 85,90,880 in the State. The elections to constitute the Panchayats for the second time were held in May 2000. A total of 54,345 members were elected to the Gram Panchayats, 2,426 to the Panchayat Samitis and 314 to the Zila Parishads.

Definition of Terms Used

It would be pertinent to explain some of the terms used in the book for they convey different meanings to different people.

Local self-government means elected local bodies created under the law and vested with specified powers and responsibilities in the administration of local public affairs including planning and development and raising of resources through taxation and other means to meet the expenses related thereto. It is a sub-unit of the State at the local level.

Decentralisation means transferring of political and administrative powers and functions from higher level governments to lower level authorities. Decentralisation is essential for making local government an effective instrument of decision-making. It confers local autonomy, improves administrative capabilities, sharpens the ability for planning and development and mobilises necessary resources – human as well as material – to implement the plans.

Decentralisation is necessary because the problems that people face are hierarchic in nature: a large number of their problems are essentially local which should be resolved locally using the local resources by the people concerned. If local problems are handled by outside agencies no matter how sincere they are, people get used to looking to others and never take responsibility on their own shoulders.

Decentralisation reaches its acme of perfection when the people are drawn into its fold and are empowered. If it is limited to the elected leaders it is deemed to be "partial *decentralisation*". When all sections of the population are enabled to participate in the local affairs of a community, then *decentralisation* is said to be total. *Democratic decentralisation* signifies the quest for a participatory and community approach and the epithet "democratic" only reinforces and underlines the democratic values, purposes, approaches and styles of governance.

People's participation means involvement of the people in conceptualisation, planning, execution, monitoring and evaluation of all activities that concerns them. It includes sharing the benefits of development on equitable basis. Since participation requires increased influence and control, it also simultaneously calls for an increased empowerment in economic, social and political terms. The development programmes and projects, which are financially dependent on the government assistance usually have a shorter life unless the people for whom they are meant actively participate in them. This fact has been stressed in the successive plan documents of the Government of India. According to the Sixth Five Year Plan document "the planning process in a democratic country can acquire fuller meaning and depth if the people not only associate themselves in planning for their development but also participate consciously in plan implementation."

Outline of the Book

The book is divided into seven chapters, each dealing with a specific theme.

Chapter one gives a broad overview of the genesis of Panchayati Raj System in the country. It also highlights the importance and contribution of the rural sector in our economy and how it needs to be developed to sustain itself.

Chapter two focuses on Panchayati Raj in Haryana. It traces the history of Panchayats in the State and exposes the merits and demerits of local governance. The chapter analyses the salient features of Haryana Panchayati Raj Act, 1994, the working of Panchayats, their powers, functions and financial resources.

Chapter three deals with the process of elections, the election machinery and the role of various agencies to ensure a free and fair elections which is essential in a democratic system of governance.

Chapter four is a case study of Panchayat elections held in 2000. It analyses the Panchayat elections in detail and also covers various steps initiated by the Election Commission to ensure a free and fair elections.

Chapter five deals with the emerging leadership pattern in Panchayats. Data of more than twenty-five thousand elected representatives has been analysed. It highlights the socio-economic background and also discusses their role in the emerging scenario.

Chapter six discusses the capacity and capability of Panchayati Raj Institutions to implement poverty alleviation programmes. It analyses in detail the implementation of JRY in one of the districts in the State and the lessons to be learnt.

Chapter seven is the concluding chapter which gives a summary of the findings of the study and also suggests certain measures to enable Panchayats to emerge as true institutions of democratic decentralisation.

Concluding Remarks

The scenario of Panchayati Raj Institutions painted above applies to Haryana too. Differences if any lie in the hues not in the intensity of the tone. This was one of the reasons why we decided to conduct our study in Haryana and go into the depth of the problems. Since this book focuses on Haryana, we do not propose to go into the details of the scenario of Panchayati Raj Institutions in the State in this introductory chapter. But we would like to state that picture painted here is not designed to find faults but to indicate the directions in which future policies and programmes to strengthen local self-government in rural parts of the country should move.

We are convinced that India would remain rural for a long time to come. And when its rural character changes, it will not be on west European and American lines. India will be a country of small towns emerging from the transformation of today's villages into better villages which R.P. Misra, one of the authorities on rural development calls micropolises. We are also convinced that there is no substitute to Panchayati Raj Institutions if democracy has to take deep roots in India. Even if they have failed in the past, they must succeed in future. It is not easy to establish democratic institutions in a country which has been under colonial rule for so long and which faced unprecedented challenges in the post-Independence era. We are aware of the way our Parliament and State Legislatures function. They are supposed to be the institutions that inspire respect and confidence in the average citizen. If they have failed to meet the aspiration of the people, why then blame the tiny Village Panchayats alone?

The country is passing through a transition period of societal change. The old values are dying but the new ones are yet to take roots. There is terrific confusion in the minds of the people about what is right and what is wrong. We feel that the current situation will more or less continue for another 10-15 years. One of the wonderful things about democracy is that self-correcting mechanisms are built in it. Job of academicians and researchers is to analyse the situation and suggest measures that accord with the cultural ethos of the society in question and globally accepted norms of democratic values. Deviations from such norms have to be highlighted and new directions indicated. This is what this little book proposes to do.

REFERENCES

Government of India, *Constitution 73rd Amendment Act, 1993*.

Haryana Government, *Haryana Panchayati Raj Act, 1994*.

Jain, S.P. 'The Gram Sabha: Gateway to Grassroots Democracy', *Journal of Rural Development*, Vol. 16, Oct.-Dec., 1997.

Malviya, H.D. *Village Panchayats in India*, All India Congress Committee, New Delhi, 1956.

Misra, R.P. *Million Cities of India*, New Delhi: Sustainable Development Foundation, 1998.

Misra, R.P. *District Planning*, Concept Publishing Company, 1990, New Delhi, 1990. See also *Million Cities of India*, Ibid.

Mishra, Suresh, *Popular Participation in Rural Development*, HIPA, Gurgaon, 1997.

Mishra, S.N. 'Decentralised Planning for Rural Development,' *Kurukshetra*, Vol. 48, No. 5, Feb. 2000.

Report of the Team for the Study of Community Development and Extension Service, New Delhi, 1957.

Report of the Committee on Panchayati Raj Institutions, Department of Rural Development, Ministry of Agriculture, 1978.

Sundaram, K.V. *Decentralised Multilevel Planning*, Concept Publishing Company, New Delhi, 1997.

2

PANCHAYATI RAJ IN HARYANA

HISTORICAL ROOTS

Before the advent of the British rule in India, the rural areas in Haryana had a traditional system of Bhaichara Panchayats (Community Councils). These panchayats did not derive their structure, roles and functions from any statute or any written law. They had a strong traditional base, and were functional for maintenance, adaptation, resource mobilisation and tension management. The land owning caste groups dominated these institutions.[1]

In the early stages of British rule it was the logic of events and of necessity, which was mainly responsible for propping up a system of local administration. The demand for democratic decentralisation came from the educated elite who wanted a share in the exercise of power and patronage. It was limited to local bodies and municipalities and based on the principle that local needs must be met by local taxation.[2] However, later on during the British rule besides the operation of the traditional Panchayats, the statutory Panchayats and District Boards which were created in 1884, consisted of officials and non-officials, appointed and nominated members. The Deputy Commissioner used to be the Chairman of the District Boards. However, this institution was gradually democratised by introducing the element of election. The genesis of statutory Panchayats in this area during the British Raj could be traced to the Punjab Village Panchayat Act of 1912 which was enacted for setting up Village Panchayats as judicial organs and not as units of local self government.[3] This Act was followed by another Act of 1921.

The enactments of the British were intended more for propaganda than for solid work and they utterly failed in establishing Panchayats to any extent or creating response among the villagers. The Panchayats so created did not have effective powers. The District Collector had complete control over the Panchayats. The 1939 Panchayat Act superseded the earlier Acts and conferred among others wide judicial powers both civil and criminal on the Panchayats. Efforts were also made to improve the financial resources of Panchayats through government grants equal to the judicial fees and fines credited by the Panchayats to the government treasury. Panchayats were also allowed to levy taxes in their respective areas with the previous sanction of the government. To look after the Panchayats a separate department was created.

POST-INDEPENDENCE DEVELOPMENTS (1947-65)

After Independence, the 1939 Act was replaced by the Panjab Gram Panchayat Act of 1952, which envisaged the constitution of Gram Panchayats each with a membership of five to nine. The election of the members was on the basis of adult franchise and the people directly elected the Sarpanch. The Gram Sabha was to meet twice a year. The term of the Panchayats was for a period of five years. The Act provided that the Gram Panchayat shall meet atleast once a month and the majority of the panches shall form a quorum. For every Gram Panchayat or a group of Panchayats there was a Gram Sachiv who was appointed by the government.[4]

The Gram Panchayats were entrusted with a number of administrative duties. They were also given certain civil, revenue and judicial functions such as suits for recovery of movable property, suits for compensation etc. The Panchayats had the power of taxation as well. They could impose a house tax, tax on profession, trade fees for registration of animals, water rate, etc.

The Government exercised ample control over the Gram Panchayats. The Deputy Commissioner or the SDO had the power to suspend the execution of any resolution or order of the Gram Panchayat. The Director was also vested with the power to suspend or remove any Panch on specified grounds. Moreover, if in the opinion of the Government, a Gram

Panchayat was incompetent to perform or persistently made default in the performance of the duties imposed on it by or under this or any other Act, the Government had the powers to supersede or suspend a Panchayat.

This was the situation which existed until 1960's, when the new Panchayati Raj System came into operation after the enactment of Panjab Panchayat Samitis and Zila Parishads Act, 1961 and amendments to the Panjab Gram Panchayat Act, 1952. The new institutional pattern that emerged was the one that was suggested by the Balwantrai Mehta study team. It was a three-tier structure with Gram Panchayat at the village level, Panchayat Samiti at the Block and Zila Parishad at the district level.

PANCHAYATI RAJ IN THE NEW STATE OF HARYANA

Haryana became a separate State in 1966. At that time, even though the system of Panchayati Raj did exist, in the State it had not taken deep roots. All local governments were controlled by the State Government and as such the Panchayati Raj institutions were not autonomous in the real sense. Until 1973, the State had three-tier system. In 1972 the Maru Singh Ad-hoc Committee on Panchayati Raj recommended a two-tier system consisting of Village Panchayats and Block Samitis. The Zila Parishads were abolished. These recommendations were implemented by the State Government in 1973. The Committee was of the view that there was unnecessary over lapping of functions between Zila Parishad and Panchayat Samiti and, therefore, the former should be abolished and its functions added on to the functions already assigned statutorily to Panchayat Samiti. Since then, Haryana has had only two-tier Panchayati Raj System.[5]

The working of Panchayats in the State ever since their formation has not been very encouraging. Panchayats did not emerge as viable institutions of local governance and due to the abolition of the Zila Parishad, the structural and institutional aspect of PRI's weakened further. As a result of this and due to the small size of the State, the Panchayats were over shadowed by State level politicians and bureaucracy. In general there had been a tendency to curtail the powers and fuctions of the PRIs and the position of the elected representatives had been undermined. Instead of devolution of powers, mechanisms were evolved to centralize authority in the State bureaucracy and political leadership. The Panchayats continued to exist but not as real instruments of economic development and social change at the grassroots level.

A number of Gram Panchayats and Panchayat Samitis were superseded and suspended. Fresh elections to reconstitute these bodies were not held on time. Financially too they were weak and had to depend on the government for funds. Apart from the bureaucratic and political strangulation from which the PRIs suffered, the Panchayats did not represent all sections of the society. Most of them were controlled by the well off sections of the rural society leaving the poor and marginalized high and dry. The scheduled castes failed to acquire a foothold in the rural power structure and the representation of the women was very poor, if at all. To further accentuate these problems, people in general were apathetic; they did not come to meetings of the Gram Sabhas as and when called. Cases where meetings were held only on paper were not rare. A strong nexus between the elected representatives and the local level bureaucracy kept the Gram Sabhas defunct for all practical purposes.

The Panchayati Raj System in Haryana could not acquire the status and dignity of a viable and responsive forum to discuss, plan and solve people's problems at the grassroots level. By early 1990's the situation had gone so bad that it called for immediate change to revitalise these bodies. Let us mention here that the situation detailed above was not peculiar to Haryana, it prevailed almost all over the country. One of the responses was to go to the roots of the problem and initiate such changes in the Constitution itself that no State government could take away the powers from the Panchayati Raj institutions. Shri Rajiv Gandhi, the then Prime Minister of India took a lead and proposed a three-tier system of government: Central, State and local (city municipalities and Village Panchayats).

The 73rd Constitutional Amendment Act was passed by the Parliament and it came into effect on April 24, 1993. Accordingly, the States were directed to amend or repeal their existing laws, to conform to the new provisions of the Constitution in this regard within one year from the commencement of the Act.

The Government of Haryana repealed the Panjab Gram Panchayat Act, 1952 and the Panjab Panchayat Samitis and Zila Parishads Act, 1961 and a new Act called the Haryana Panchayati Raj Act was passed in 1994.

HARYANA PANCHAYATI RAJ ACT, 1994

The Haryana Panchayati Raj Act enacted in 1994 provided for the constitution of Gram Panchayats, Panchayat Samitis and Zila Parishads for better administration of the rural areas. According to this Act, the tenure of all Panchayati Raj bodies is five years unless dissolved earlier.[6]

The Gram Sabha

According to the Act, any village or a part of a village or group of contiguous villages with a population of not less than five hundred can constitute one or more Gram Sabha areas. In exceptional cases the population limit of 500 could be relaxed. Each Gram Sabha would have a Gram Panchayat which will consist of a Sarpanch who shall be elected by the Gram Sabha from amongst its voters by secret ballot. Further, It will have six to twenty Panchs representing different wards of the Panchayat area in a prescribed manner. The Panchs will elect an Up-Sarpanch (Vice-Sarpanch) from amongst themselves in the first meeting of the Gram Panchayat.

The Act prescribes that every Gram Panchayat shall hold two general meetings of the Gram Sabha each year, one between May 1 and June 30 and the other between November 1 and December 31. In case the Sarpanch of a Panchayat fails to hold two consecutive general meetings of the Gram Sabha on the dates fixed by the Panchayat, he shall automatically cease to hold office from the date on which the second meeting was to be held. The Block Development and Panchayat Officer shall immediately intimate the happening of such to the Director of Panchayati Raj who shall notify this fact to the Zila Parishad, Panchayat Samiti, Gram Panchayat and the Sarpanch. The Director could reinstate the Sarpanch on his showing sufficient cause for the default within a period of thirty days.

The meeting of the Gram Sabha shall be conducted and the time and place of such meeting shall be notified in advance. One-tenth of the total number of its members shall form a quorum for any meeting of the Gram Sabha. The Block Development and Panchayat Officer and the Gram Sachiv of a Gram Panchayat shall attend every general meeting of the Gram Sabha. The Gram Sabha can call every village level functionary serving in the Sabha area to attend such meetings and tender advice.

The Gram Panchayat

Representation of Weaker Sections

In order to give due representation to the weaker sections of the population including women, certain number of positions of the Sarpanches and Panches are reserved for them. The number of seats reserved for the Scheduled Castes are in the proportion to their population in each Panchayat. Those Wards, which had more people belonging to these castes are in general reserved for them. To provide representation to Scheduled Caste women, at least one-third of the total number of seats reserved for Scheduled Castes are reserved for women. Ward-wise reservation for Scheduled Caste women is done by rotation and by lots. There is a similar provision for general (unreserved) seats also.

Not less than one-third of the total number of offices of Sarpanches in the Block is also reserved for women including one-third offices of women Sarpanches from Scheduled Castes. Every Panchayat shall have one Panch belonging to Backward Classes, if their population is two per cent or more of the total population of the Sabha area and such seat is allotted to such Wards having maximum population of persons belonging to Backward Classes.

Terms of Office of Sarpanch and Up-Sarpanch

The term of office of Sarpanch and Up-Sarpanch is fixed at five years unless removed earlier. The Gram Sabha is given the power to remove the Sarpanch from his office by a majority of not less than two-thirds of the voters of the Gram Sabha present at its extraordinary general meeting attended by not less than fifty per cent of its members. Similarly, any Up-Sarpanch can be removed from his office by a two-thirds majority by the Panches of the Gram Panchayat. A meeting to remove the Up-Sarpanch shall be convened only on a requisition made to the prescribed authority by a majority of not less than one-half of the Panches.

The Director or the Deputy Commissioner concerned may suspend any Sarpanch, Up-Sarpanch or Panch where a case against him in respect of any criminal offence is under investigation, enquiry or trial if in their opinion the charges made or proceedings taken against him is likely to embarrass him in the discharge of his duties or involves moral-turpitude or defect in character. He can also be suspended or removed during the course of an enquiry for any of the reasons for which he can be removed after giving him adequate opportunity to explain. The Panch can be placed under suspension if he absents himself from meetings of the Gram Panchayat consecutively thrice.

Meetings of Gram Panchayat

The meeting of a Gram Panchayat shall be held at least twice a month at a public place within the Gram Sabha area. A majority of the Panches could requisition a meeting of the Panchayat and the Sarpanch would have to call such a meeting within three days. A simple majority of the Panches and the Sarpanch will form a quorum of Panchayat meetings. The decision of the Gram Panchayat shall be by majority and when the voting is equal, the President shall have a casting vote.

The Government will appoint a Gram Sachiv for every Gram Panchayat or group of Gram Panchayats. It shall be the duty of the Gram Sachiv to maintain accurate and up-to-date entries in accounts and record. He would look after the property of the Gram Panchayat under the general supervision of the Sarpanch and assist the Gram Panchayat in the discharge of its duties and functions.

Powers and Functions of Panchayats

Powers of Sarpanches

The Sarpanch has been vested with a number of functions and duties. He shall convene and preside over the meetings of the Gram

Sabha and Gram Panchayat. He has the general responsibility for the executive and financial administration of the Gram Panchayat. He is to exercise administrative supervision and control over the work of the staff of the Gram Panchayat and the officers and employees who may be placed at the disposal of the Gram Panchayat. The Up-Sarpanch in the absence of the Sarpanch presides over and conducts the meetings of Gram Sabha and Gram Panchayat. He also exercises such powers and performs such duties of the Sarpanch as may be delegated to him by the Sarpanch.

Duties of Gram Panchayats

The Gram Panchayat shall prepare a report on the work done during the previous year and the work proposed to be done during the following year and submit to the prescribed authority and to the Panchayat Samiti concerned. It shall be the duty of the Gram Panchayat, within the limits of the funds at its disposal, to make arrangements for meeting the requirements of people in matters by preparing annual plans for the development and annual budget for the approval of the Gram Sabha. It will mobilise relief in natural calamities and make provisions for the development and promotion of agriculture, animal husbandry, dairying and poultry, fisheries, housing, waterways, rural electrification, poverty alleviation programmes, education including primary and secondary schools. Other areas which come under the purview of the Panchayats are: rural sanitation, markets and fairs, public health and family welfare, women and child development, social welfare, welfare of the weaker sections, public distribution system, maintenance of community assets, maintenance of public parks, play grounds and any other function as may be entrusted by the Government.

Sub-Committees

Every Gram Panchayat will have the following sub-committees, namely:

(a) Production Sub-Committee for performing functions relating to agriculture production, animal husbandry, rural industries and poverty alleviation programmes,

(b) Social Justice Sub-Committee for performing functions relating to promotion of education, economic, social, cultural, sports and other interests of the Scheduled Castes, Backward Classes and other weaker sections;

(c) Amenities Sub-Committee for education, public health, public works and other functions.

Each Sub-Committee and local committee shall consist of not less than five members including Sarpanch and Up-Sarpanch. The Sarpanch is the *ex-officio* member and Chairman of Production and Amenities Committee. The Up-Sarpanch is the *ex-officio* member and Chairman of the Social Justice Committee.

Financial and Fiscal Powers

As regards, finance of the Panchayats, each Gram Panchayat shall have a Gram Fund and it should be utilised for carrying out the duties and obligations imposed on the Gram Panchayat. All grants from the Government or other local authorities shall be credited to the Gram Fund. The funds shall also consist of all donations, all taxes, duties, cesses, fine and fees imposed and realised under this Act. Income derived from common lands vested in the Gram Panchayat shall also form part of the Gram Fund.

As far as taxation is concerned, the Gram Panchayat shall impose a house tax, a duty on transfer of property in the form of surcharge on the duty imposed by the Indian Stamp Act, 1899 on instruments on sale, gift etc. and any other tax, duty or cess if so authorised by the Government. The Panchayat may also levy fees on *teh-bazari* from the shopkeepers in fairs other than cattle fair, service fee, fee for registration of animals and water ratio where water is supplied by the Gram Panchayat.

The accounts of the receipts and expenditure of every Gram Panchayat shall be made up in such form as may be prescribed and the Gram Panchayat shall make arrangements for the examination and audit of the accounts by such persons as the Government may appoint in this behalf. The Gram Sachiv shall prepare a statement of the accounts of the Gram Panchayat for each financial year, showing the income of Gram Panchayat under each head of receipt, the charges for establishment, the works undertaken, the sums expended on each work and the balance.

Dissolution of Gram Panchayats

If in the opinion of the Government, a Gram Panchayat abuses its powers or is not competent to perform or makes persistent defaults in the performance of its duties or wilfully disregards any instructions given or directions issued by the Panchayat Samiti or Zila Parishad or any other instructions issued by the competent authority, after giving the Gram Panchayats an opportunity to render explanation dissolve such Gram Panchayat. A Gram Panchayat shall be reconstituted before the expiration of a period of six months. A reconstituted Panchayat shall continue only for the remainder of the period for which the dissolved Panchayat would have continued.

Panchayat Samiti

The Haryana Panchayati Raj Act, 1994 provides for the constitution of Panchayat Samitis at the Block level. The size of the Blocks in terms of their respective population and number of Gram Panchayats included therein would be notified by the Government of the State from time to time.

Each Panchayat Samiti shall consist of :

(a) directly elected members from territorial constituencies as determined under Section 58 of thc Act. Each Panchayat Samiti shall have a Chairman and a Vice-Chairman who shall be elected by and from amongst the elected members. The number of elected members shall not be less than ten and not more than thirty.

(b) the members of Haryana Legislative Assembly representing constituencies which comprise wholly or partly the Panchayat Samiti shall be *ex-officio* members. They shall have right to vote in the meeting of the Panchayat Samiti except for the election and removal of Chairman and Vice-Chairman; and

(c) one-fifths of the total number of Sarpanches of the Gram Panchayats within the jurisdiction of the Panchayat Samiti. They shall have right to vote in the meeting of Panchayat Samiti except for election and removal of the Chairman and Vice-Chairman of the Panchayat Samiti.

To give proper representation to the weaker sections of the society and also to women, the Act provides for reservation of seats for Scheduled Castes in proportion to their total population in the area. And within the reserved seats not less than one-third of the total number of seats shall be reserved for women belonging to Scheduled Castes and such seats may be allotted by rotation and by draw of lots amongst the reserved Wards. The formula of reservation for the women would also apply to unreserved seats.

The Act provides that not less than one-third of the total number of offices of Chairpersons of Panchayat Samiti in a district shall be reserved for women including women belonging to the Scheduled Castes. One seat shall be reserved for Backward Classes and the same shall be allotted to that constituency, which has the maximum population of persons belonging to that class.

The election of Chairman and Vice-Chairman would take place in the first meeting of the newly constituted Panchayat Samiti by and from amongst its elected members. The powers of the Chairman are:

(a) to convene, preside over and conduct meetings of the Panchayat Samiti;
(b) discharge all duties imposed and exercise all the powers conferred on him;
(c) watch over the financial and executive administration of the Panchayat Samiti;
(d) submit to the Panchayat Samiti all information connected with finances and administration;
(e) exercise administrative supervision of the Block Development and Panchayat Officer for securing implementation of resolutions or decisions of the Panchayat Samiti; and

(f) the Vice-Chairman shall, in the absence of the Chairman, preside over the meetings of the Panchayat Samiti and exercise such of the powers and perform duties of the Chairman, as the Chairman may delegate to him from time to time.

The term of office of the Chairman and Vice-Chairman of a Panchayat Samiti shall be five years.

Functions and Duties

The Panchayat Samiti is required to carry out the development of the area under its jurisdiction in respect of the following matters:

(a) preparation of annual plans in respect of the schemes entrusted to it and submission to the Chief Executive Officer within a period of two months of its receipt for the consideration of the District Planning Committee;
(b) consideration and consolidation of the annual plans of all Gram Panchayat in the Block and submission of the consolidated plan to the Zila Parishad;
(c) preparation of annual budget of the Block and its submission to the Zila Parishad;
(d) arranging for relief in natural calamities;
(e) providing for and making arrangements in the area for agricultural development, land improvement and soil conservation, minor irrigation, animal husbandry, fisheries, rural housing, drinking water, maintenance of buildings and property, education, women and child development, social welfare, public distribution system, promotion of rural electrification and any other functions entrusted to it;
(f) the Panchayat Samiti shall function as the agent of the Government for the formulation and execution of the various development programmes within the area of its jurisdiction. It shall exercise supervision and control over various administrative functions of the Gram Panchayats within its area. It will also render assistance to the Gram Panchayat for the implementation of development schemes which are beyond the powers of the Gram Panchayats to execute.

In order to discharge its functions effectively, the Panchayat Samiti shall appoint the following Committees:

(a) General Committee,
(b) Finance, Audit and Planning Committee, and
(c) Social Justice Committee.

Each Committee shall consist of such number of members not exceeding six including the Chairman. The election of the members of the committees and their functioning would be regulated by the Samiti.

Conduct of Business

A meeting of the Panchayat Samiti could be ordinary or special. The quorum of an ordinary meeting shall be one-third of the members, and of the special meeting, one-half of the number of members actually serving for the time being. The Panchayat Samities would ordinarily meet at least six times in each year and not more than two months should be allowed to elapse between any two successive meetings.

The Executive power of a Panchayat Samiti vests in its Chairman and the Executive Officer. The Executive Officer shall implement the resolutions of the Samiti and report to the Samiti the progress made and also furnish such information as it may require from time to time.

Financial and Fiscal Powers

Panchayat Samities have the same taxation power, which the Legislature of the State has under the Constitution of India subject to general direction and control of the Government. It can also levy user fee on patients who benefit from public hospitals, dispensaries, schools, markets, supply and storage of water, preservation and reclamation of soil and fairs, agricultural shows and industrial exhibitions held within its area.

Every Panchayat Samiti shall have a fund called the 'Samiti Fund' and all proceeds of all taxes, cesses and fees imposed by it, all funds allocated to it, all incomes arising from various other sources including rents and profits, all sums contributed to the

Fund by the Central or, State Government or any local authority, and other grants and proceeds shall be credited to the Samiti Fund. All payments with respect to the work executed by the Samiti shall be payed out of the Samiti Fund. The Committee of Finance and Taxation would submit to the Samiti an estimate of income and expenditure for the ensuing financial year. The Budget shall consist of two parts :

(a) the budget of the Community Development Block; and
(b) the funds transferred from other departments and income derived by the Samiti from other sources.

The Panchayat Samiti shall consider both the parts of the budget and approve it with or without any modifications. The budget shall then go to the Zila Parishad for its approval.

Supervision of Panchayat Samiti

The Chief Executive Officer (CEO) of the Samiti shall have power to inspect any immovable property within the limits of his jurisdiction occupied or vested in any Panchayat Samiti. He can by order call and inspect any document which may be in the possession or under the control of any Panchayat Samiti. The CEO can order the Panchayat Samiti to furnish such statements, accounts, reports as he may think fit.

The Government shall advice, supervise and co-ordinate the functions of the Panchayat Samities. The Government shall have powers to issue directives to Panchayat Samities with respect to the efficient performance of their duties, which shall be binding on the Panchayat Samities. It can also give advice, coordinate and consolidate development plans, secure the execution of plans, projects, schemes, advice Panchayat Samities on all matters relating to development activities. The Government shall have the authority to call for any information, statement or record from a Panchayat Samiti and can also cancel any resolution passed by a Panchayat Samiti if in their opinion the resolution is not legally passed or is in excess or abuse of the powers conferred by or under this Act or any other law or is contrary to the interests of the public or likely to cause, waste or damage of Samiti Fund or property of a Panchayat Samiti.

If a Panchayat Samiti is not competent to perform or persistently makes default in the performance of the duties imposed upon it by or under this or any other Act the Government may *suo motu* or on a report received in this behalf and after giving an opportunity to the Panchayat Samiti to show cause and dissolve such Panchayat Samiti. When a Panchayat Samiti is dissolved then all members of the Panchayat Samiti shall from the date of the notification vacate the office, and all powers and duties of the Panchayat Samiti, until the Panchayat Samiti is reconstituted be exercised and performed by such person or persons as the Government may appoint in this behalf. The Government also has powers to enquire into the affairs of Panchayat Samiti in regard to any matter concerning it.

Zila Parishad

Each district will have a Zila Parishad with jurisdiction extending to the whole of the district, its Panchayat Samities and Gram Panchayats. It however excludes municipalities and cantonments. The members of the Zila Parishad are directly elected from the electoral Wards. The Chairpersons of the Panchayat Samities within the district, *ex-officio* members, the members of the Lok Sabha, and State legislature whose constituencies fall within the district wholly or partly and a President and Vice-President who shall be elected by and from amongst the elected members of the Zila Parishad, shall constitute the Zila Parishad. The *ex-officio* members of the Zila Parishad shall have right to vote in the meetings of the Zila Parishad but they cannot participate in the vote of confidence against the President or the Vice-President of the Parishad. The Zila Parishad shall consist of not more than thirty and not less than ten directly elected members depending on the population of the district. 40,000 eligible voters would form a Ward and elect one member. The election would be direct. As in the case of Gram Panchayats and Panchayat Samities, seats are reserved for the Scheduled Castes, Women and Backward Classes in the Zila Parishad too.

The President and Vice-President of the Zila Parishad are elected by and from amongst its elected members in the first meeting of the Zila Parishad. The President of Zila Parishad :

1. convenes, presides and conducts meetings of the Zila Parishad;
2. he has access to records;
3. he discharges all assigned duties, and exercises all the powers conferred on him;
4. watches over the financial and executive administration of the Zila Parishad;
5. exercises administrative supervision over the Chief Executive Officer for securing implementation of resolutions or decisions of the Zila Parishad; and
6. The Vice-President, in the absence of the President, presides over the meetings of the Zila Parishad and exercises powers delegated to him by the President.

Ordinarily, the Zila Parishad meets at least six times in a year at an interval of two months. The quorum of an ordinary meeting is one-third of the members and for the special meeting, it is one-half of the number of members in position. The Additional Deputy Commissioner is the *ex-officio* Chief Executive Officer of the Zila Parishad. There is provision for the appointment of Accounts Officers if the Zila Parishad requires. For day-to-day work, one of senior district level officers functions as a Deputy Chief Executive Officer-cum-Secretary. Zila Parishad has its own office which is headed by the Chief Executive Officer.

The CEO supervises the execution of all works of the Zila Parishad and Panchayat Samities and has administrative control over the officers working under him. He attends the meetings of the Zila Parishad and is authorized to attend the meeting of any committee but does not have the right to move any resolution or to vote. The Accounts Officer advises the Zila Parishad in matters of finance and is answerable to the Zila Parishad. The Deputy Chief Executive Officer-cum-Secretary assists the Chief Executive Officer in performance of his duties.

Duties and Functions

A Zila Parishad advises, supervises and co-ordinates the functions of the Panchayat Samities in the district. It has the power to co-ordinate and consolidate development plans prepared by Panchayat Samities; secure the execution of plans, projects, schemes; advise government on the allocation of work among Gram Panchayats and Panchayat Samities and co-ordinate their work; and examine and approve the budget of Panchayat Samities in the manner laid down; and levy contribution from the funds of the Panchayat Samities in the district. The Zila Parishad can undertake the construction, maintenance or repair of any work or the management of any institution within its jurisdiction.

The Zila Parishad may constitute committees necessary for executing its functions. The President of a Zila Parishad shall be the *ex-officio* Chairman of each Committee and the Chief Executive Officer shall be the *ex-officio* Secretary of every such committee. The Zila Parishad may frame regulations relating to election of members of committees, conduct of business and other related matters.

In addition to the movable or immovable property acquired by a Zila Parishad, every building or other work constructed by a Zila Parishad out of the Zila Parishad Fund, any land or property vesting in the Government when transferred to a Zila Parishad for public purposes, any land or other property vesting in any other Panchayat when transferred to the Zila Parishad by that Panchayat shall vest in the Zila Parishad.

Each Zila Parishad shall have a fund called the "Zila Parishad Fund". The proceeds of any tax, cess, toll or fee imposed; the sale proceeds of all dust, dirt, dung, refuse; 5 per cent to 10 per cent of the funds allotted to a district as grants-in-aid; all sums received by way of loans from the State Government; all sums received by way of gift or contribution by the Zila Parishad shall be paid into and form part of the Zila Parishad Fund.

Subject to general direction and control of the Government, a Zila Parishad may, with the prior approval of the Government, impose any tax, levy fee for the use of or benefits derived from public hospitals, dispensaries, schools, markets, the supply and storage of water and preservation and reclamation of soil and drainage. The Zila Parishad shall prepare a budget of its estimated receipts and disbursements and submit it to the Government. The accounts are to be maintained in the prescribed manner and the audit of the account shall be carried out by the Auditor General of India

Suspension and Dissolution

The Government or any other officer appointed may inspect the offices or premises of or works taken up by Zila Parishad and examine the books of accounts, registers and other documents concerned. If in the opinion of the Government, a Zila Parishad exceeds or abuses its powers or is incompetent to perform or makes persistent defaults in the performance of the duties imposed on or functions entrusted to it under any provision of this Act, the Government may after enquiry and after giving the Zila Parishad an opportunity of rendering an explanation, dissolve the Zila Parishad. If a Zila Parishad is dissolved all the powers and duties of the Zila Parishad shall during the period of dissolution be exercised and performed by such person or persons as the Government may from time to time appoint in that behalf. The Government may cancel any resolution passed by a Zila Parishad or a Committee if in its opinion, such resolution is not legally passed or is in excess or abuse of the powers conferred under this Act or any other law or is contrary to the interest of the public or likely to cause waste or damage of Zila Parishad Fund or of the property of a Zila Parishad.

The Government may suspend any President or Vice-President or Member as the case may be where a case against him/her in respect of any criminal offence is under investigation, enquiry or trial and if in the opinion of the Government, the charge made or proceedings taken against him/her are likely to embarrass him/her in the discharge of duties or involves moral turpitude or defect of character.

Joint Works and Undertakings

A Gram Panchayat, Panchayat Samiti and Zila Parishad may contribute towards any work, measure, institution or service from which the area under the jurisdiction of a Gram Panchayat, Panchayat Samiti or Zila Parishad benefits although such works institution or service is undertaken or maintained outside such area and contribute funds to any such work or institution any sum as may appear to the Gram Panchayat, Panchayat Samiti or Zila Parishad reasonable having regard to the extent of benefits derived therefrom.

PANCHAYATI RAJ SYSTEM : A CRITIQUE

The system of Panchayati Raj had not been functioning efficiently and effectively because of a number of reasons. One of them is the lack of real power to do anything meaningful. In theory these local bodies have all the powers they need, but in practice, they have very little. They are still controlled and manipulated by the bureaucracy. In Haryana, the State Government in the recent past has made serious efforts to empower the Panchayats by not only involving them in planning and project formulation, but also in the execution the works. It has tried to activate the Panchayats by vesting them with various functional and administrative roles.

In 1999, the Chief Minister of the State launched a very innovative programme called *'Sarkar Aapke Dwar'* (government at your door) to empower the Panchayati Raj institutions. As a part of this movement, the development programmes at village and Block level are decided by the Chief Minister on the basis of the priorities set by the Panchayats. At the time of oath taking ceremony of Panches and Sarpanches at Jind on April 23, 2000, the Chief Minister announced a package of devolution plan for the newly elected Chairmen of Zila Parishad and the Panchayat Samities as well as for the Sarpanches and Panches of Panchayats. The level of authority of the Sarpanches was enhanced substantially to enable them to incur expenses for development works. Certain supervisory functions of different departments were also delegated to the Panchayats.

The next phase of strengthening of the Panchayati Raj institutions came with the concept of direct implementation of development works by the Panchayats themselves instead of the works being executed by different Government agencies without the knowledge or concurrence of the Panchayats. Let us discuss some of these powers and responsibilities that have been recently transferred :

1. The primary and middle schools have been brought under the direct control of the Zila Parishads. These schools will function under the supervision of the Zila Parishads. In order to encourage sports and games at the District and Block level all such competitions will be conducted by the Zila Parishad and the Panchayat Samiti under the supervision of the officers of the Sports Department. The Sports Department will provide financial aid to the Panchayats to conduct such competitions.
2. The selection of beneficiaries of age old pension, widow pension and handicap pension will be done on the recommendations of the Gram Panchayat and such pension will be disbursed in the presence of the Sarpanch or Panch of the concerned Gram Panchayat.
3. In the Selection Committee of Anganwadi workers and Anganwadi helpers, a woman member of the concerned Gram Panchayat will be a member. The distribution of nutritious food at the Anganwadi centres will be done in the presence of the Sarpanch or women Panch. A woman member nominated by the Zila Parishad or Panchayat Samiti can inspect the Anganwadi centres and is authorised to take the Project Officer and the CDPO on such inspections.
4. The time schedule of Haryana Transport rural route buses will be decided in consultation with the Panchayat Samiti and Zila Parishad. In case, a Gram Panchayat desires to run buses on local routes then priority will be given to the Gram Panchayat in issue of permits on such routes.
5. Similarly, in the case of preparation of ration cards and allotment of ration depots in the village the Gram Panchayat will be consulted. The Gram Panchayats can

inspect any ration depot and the distribution of ration items will be done in the presence of the Sarpanch or the Panch. In case of shortcomings in public distribution system, the Gram Panchayat will send its report to the Controller of Food and Civil Supplies. The facilities of non-conventional energy sources will be provided to the beneficiaries on the advice of the Panchayat Samities. The Village Panchayat can make their recommendations to the Panchayat Samities.

6. To ensure life and liberty of an individual and save him from arbitrary actions of the police, it is mandatory for the SHO of the concerned police station to inform the concerned village Sarpanch in case any person of a village has been taken into police custody. The Gram Panchayats will also lend their full cooperation to the concerned departments in checking the theft of electricity and water meant for irrigation.
7. To enforce accountability and ensure presence of the local level officials it is provided that the Agriculture Development Officer when on tour will enter his attendance in the register maintained by the Panchayat. He will identify the beneficiaries of various schemes to be implemented on the advice of the Panchayats. The concerned Panchayat Samiti will enter remarks on three items in the confidential report of the Agriculture Development Officer and the Circle Agriculture Officer. Similarly, the Zila Parishad will comment on three items in the Confidential Report of the Assistant Director (Agriculture).
8. The employees of the Community Health Centres, Primary Health Centres and Sub-Centres will forward their leave application through the respective Panchayats. The concerned Panchayats will also enter their remarks on four points in the ACR's of the employees of these three concerned health centres. The State Government has provided a grant of Rs. 5000 for each Panchayat in the State under the Referral Transport for Poor Families scheme under which monetary assistance is given for taking pregnant women to the health centre

for safe delivery. It is to be observed that the Panchayats have not been able to utilise this amount. Inspite of this scheme all the Panchayats of Kurukshetra district could not spend a single rupee under this head and the whole amount was returned to the Government unused. The Panchayats should take advantage of such schemes meant for women and ensure that the pregnant women get the much needed relief.

9. The Gram Panchayats have been responsible for the maintenance of buildings of veterinary clinics for which the concerned departments will provide the funds. The leave application of the employees of these centres is to be forwarded by the Gram Panchayats.
10. Similarly, the employees of the water supply scheme based on tubewell system will sign their attendance in the register maintained by the Village Panchayat. Based on the attendance report of the Gram Panchayat, the salary of such employees will be paid.

Some how the centrally sponsored schemes have not come fully under the purview of the Panchayati Raj System. These schemes are implemented through special agencies created at the district level or through informal and formal organisations established over the years and financed by the Central Ministries directly. In some cases the local bodies have been associated but they are merely performing agency functions with no decisive role clearly assigned to them in the preparation and implementation of the schemes.

In particular mention may be made of the District Rural Development Agencies (DRDA), which are operating as instruments of the Central Government for the planning and implementation of many programmes and schemes related to the subjects that fall in the purview of the Panchayats. These agencies have not been integrated with the new set-up as has been done in some of the States where DRDA's have been placed under the control of the Panchayats. It is important to ensure that the local bodies function as institutions of self-government and all impediments to the realisation of this are removed.

GRAM VIKAS SAMITI

In order to accelerate the pace of rural development and to bring about quality and transparency the State Government has constituted "Gram Vikas Samities". It is argued that these Samities would not only ensure that development of rural areas was accelerated but also execute development works at much competitive and lower rates. It is also hoped that the constitution of these committees would bring down corruption in the execution of developmental works and would guarantee that works were completed in time and as per approved specifications and quality. The funds thus saved could then be utilised for other developmental works.

As far as the structure of the Samiti is concerned, the Sarpanch of the Panchayat is its Chairman. Four Panches of the Panchayat are its members. Among the four one is woman, other a Scheduled Caste and another a Backward Panch. In addition to these members, the Samiti consists of an ex-serviceman and two other members nominated by the Gram Sabha.

The funds received from the State Government are deposited in a Bank in a separate account called "Gram Vikas Nidhi". The account is operated by the Sarpanch and two other members of the Committee. Further, all developmental funds received from the State Government and other agencies is also credited into the Gram Vikas Nidhi. The funds are utilised by the Samiti to carry out developmental works. As far as management of funds/grants received from the Central Government is concerned, it continues to be received by the Panchayats as before.

While analysing the powers vested with the Samities, we find that it takes over all the developmental works entrusted to the Panchayats by the 73rd Constitutional Amendment Act. All the Panchayat works executed by different agencies will be carried out by the Gram Vikas Samiti. The engineers will only provide the technical advice. Procedures to carry out the works have also been laid down. A representative of department to which the work belongs is co-opted by the committee. For example, if the Gram Vikas Samiti has to construct a school building, the headmaster of the concerned school will be a member of the Samiti.

This decision of the Government has become controversial. According to reports published in *The Tribune* "the decision of the Haryana Government to set up Gram Vikas Samities has not gone down well with the members of the local bodies. While resentment is brewing among Panches and Sarpanches who have clandestinely held meetings in some districts to devise an action plan to counter the move, they contend that they cannot openly come out against the 'unreasonable' decision against the Government. In fact with the Samiti's coming into effect there will be very little we can do. Our powers have been scuttled and a private body has been put at the helm of affairs" said a Panch. The Gram Sabha and the Panchayats feel that the provision of grants to the Gram Vikas Samiti, cuts at the very basis of the Gram Panchayats, which are Constitutional authorities.[7]

It is also felt that there is no justification in installing people who are not elected representatives of the people. It amounts to bypassing the Constitution and its provisions. The decision may dilute the authority and power of the elected bodies and may be in violation of the Constitutional provisions. In the days to come the constitution of Gram Vikas Samities may weaken the Panchayati Raj System in the State. It is bound to create confusion and has created two centres of power, one at the level of the Gram Panchayat and the other at the level of the Gram Vikas Samiti.

The Constitution of the Gram Vikas Samities parallel to the Panchayats has also drawn the attention of the Central Government. The Prime Minister in a letter addressed to all the Chief Ministers has advised them not to create parallel bodies to the Panchayats. The Panchayats are Constitutional bodies bestowed with certain powers and functions relating to the development of their areas. It is necessary to empower and strengthen these local bodies, which are instruments of democratic decentralisation and not create parallel bodies, which encroach upon the powers and functions of these bodies.

But there is a positive side of the move too. The Gram Panchayats are not very effective bodies. Small committees in which majority of the members are Panches and whose Chairman is the Sarpanch can perform better. The arrangement would however be more democratic and meaningful, if the Gram Sabhas are revived and they become the real decision-making bodies. The resolutions passed by the Gram Sabhas could be whetted by the Panchayats, and the execution of the work could be entrusted to the Gram Vikas Samities.

There is another point worth consideration. Let the Gram Sabhas become the general bodies (equivalent to State Legislatures at the village level), Gram Panchayats the executive councils (equivalent to the ministries in the State), and the Gram Vikas Samities, the bodies which carry out the tasks approved by the Gram Panchayat. This may reduce the dependence of the Gram Panchayats on the bureaucracy as the execution of the works is in the hands of the bureaucracy It would be easier to hold the Gram Vikas Samiti responsible for any wrong action than the local bureaucracy.

Out of 6,019 Gram Panchayats in Haryana, nearly 5,857 of them had constituted Gram Vikas Samities at the time of the survey. The others were in the process of passing resolutions to this effect.

Financial Resources[8]

Budget, Accounts and Audit

The budget estimates are prepared by Gram Sabha at its Sawani meeting and thereafter is approved by the Gram Panchayat with or without modifications. The budget estimates of Panchayat Samiti framed by the Finance, Audit and Planning Committee are considered and approved by the Panchayat Samiti and then submitted to Zila Parishad for approval. The Zila Parishad submits its annual budget estimates to the State Government for approval.

The Gram Fund is operated by the Sarpanch and in his absence by Up-Sarpanch or any other Panch specifically authorised by the Gram Panchayat. No amount can be withdrawn without the express permission of the Gram Panchayat through a resolution passed for the purpose. The respective Executive Officers and Chief Executive Officers are to ensure that proper accounts of all receipts and expenditure on behalf of the Panchayat Samiti or Zila Parishad are maintained. It would be their responsibility to render such accounts to the Panchayat Samiti or Zila Parishad as and when required.

Internal Check

Audit of accounts ensures that the expenses are incurred by a proper authority observing the canons of financial propriety. It has also to watch the financial interests of the taxpayer and to control wastage, unauthorized payments, and proper use of the stocks and stores. For this purpose, the audit of the accounts of all receipts and expenditure of every Gram Panchayat is to be conducted once in two years and that of Panchayat Samiti and Zila Parishad every year by an officer appointed by the relevant department of the Government. Every Gram Panchayat, Panchayat Samiti, or Zila Parishad has to produce the relevant records to the auditors for conducting the audit.

The audit of accounts of the Panchayats in the State is very slow and tedious process especially in the case of Gram Panchayats. According to the Annual Report 1998-99 of Local Audit Department, out of 110 Panchayat Samities in the State, the audit of 93 Samities was conducted during the year. As against this, out of the 6,441 auditable Gram Panchayats, the accounts of only 1,653 Panchayats were audited. The audit of all the Gram Panchayats could not be completed during the year due to paucity of audit staff.[9]

Numerous cases of embezzlement/misappropriation, and irregular, excess, avoidable and wasteful expenditure were detected in the accounts of various Panchayats. The non-observance of the rules, and lack of proper supervision and control by the administrative authorities, were found to be the main causes. The amounts under audit objection are given in Table 2.1. It is of some interest to note that embezzlement/misappropriations of funds is much larger in the Gram Panchayats than in the Panchayat Samities, while irregular, excess and wasteful expenditure is much higher in Panchayat Samities than in Gram Panchayats.

Table 2.1 : Embezzlement and Wasteful Expenditure

(in Lacs of Rupees)

Institution	Embezzlement/Mis-appropriations	Irregular, excess, avoidable and wasteful expenditures
Panchayat Samities	0.91	41.69
Gram Panchayats	24.48	3.33
Total	25.39	45.02

Source : Annual Report 1998-99, Local Audit Department, Haryana.

The Panchayat Samities showed heavy outstanding amounts against temporary advances awaited adjustment. Arrears of taxes, rents and other levies were also found to be fairly large indicating that local bodies were not serious about augmenting their resources through taxes. The unadjusted temporary advances amounted to Rs.12.70 lakhs and the arrears of taxes to Rs. 160.34 lakhs. Apparently, there was inadequate internal check.

For an overview of the irregularities found in PRI's certain extracts from the Annual Report of 1998-99 of the Local Audit Department, Haryana are reproduced below:

Zila Parishad, Panipat

Rs. 2,50,910 were drawn vide cheque No. 866647 dated 20.7.95 being the cost of Nova Ambassador Car (Diesel) and paid in advance to M/s Hindustan Motors Ltd. Delhi (Head Office at Calcutta) through Demand Draft dated 21.7.95 but Zila Parishad failed to take timely delivery of Car for months together and in the meantime rates were revised/enhanced. The delivery of car was ultimately taken by paying Rs. 2,73,021 which resulted into avoidable payment of Rs. 22,111.

Panchayat Samiti, Sadhaura

The closing balance of Personal Ledger Account on 12.9.96 as recorded at page 92 of cash book was worked out to Rs. 1,93,364 whereas Cash Book balance was worked out as Rs. 1,71,621. The discrepancy of Rs. 21,743 in the balance of Cash Book and Personal Ledger Account was not reconciled.

Panchayat Samiti, Nahar

The cash book closing balance on 30.5.97 was Rs. 73,852.70. Where against opening balance on 1.6.97 - 17.6.97 was taken as Rs. 61,382.90. The opening balance was thus less taken by Rs. 12,469.80. Rs. 4,769.60 were later deposited by Sh. Karam Singh, Accountant without making any correction in the opening balance. The balance amount of Rs. 7,700 remained still unrecovered and apparently seemed to have been embezzled.

Panchayat Samiti, Bahadurgarh

Rs. 25,000 paid to the Indian Red Cross Society, District Jhajjar Branch vide Voucher. No. 17 of 3/98 did not constitute a valid charge on the Samiti Fund.

Panchayat Samiti, Barwala

Rs. 35,000 were sanctioned as grant-in-aid to Gram Panchayat Panihari vide Samiti resolution No. 5(4) dated 24.3.98 for the construction of Cow Ghat. The grant-in-aid amount was paid vide Voucher No. 29 of 3/98. As per item 2 of Schedule 'A' under Rule 74 of Panchayat Samiti and Zila Parishad Budget, Accounts and Audit Rules, 1996, Samiti was competent to sanction such grants only upto an amount of Rs. 10,000. The Samiti had thus exceeded its powers of financial sanction in violation of rules.

Panchayat Samiti, Mandi Dabwali

Rs. 22,074 were spent on the Sarpanch/Panches *sammelan* against the prescribed limit of Rs. 1500 fixed as per instructions issued vide Haryana Government Development and Panchayat Department Memo No. GA-81/24073-162 dated 13.5.81. Thus, Rs. 20,574 were spent irregularly by the Samiti.

Panchayat Samiti, Rania

Rs. 24,000 were spent on the purchase of stationery vide Voucher No. 9 of 4/97 against the prescribed limit of Rs. 5,000 per annum under Rule 7 of Appendix 'A' of the Haryana Panchayati Raj, Financial Budget, Accounts, Audit Taxation and Works Rules, 1996. Thus, Rs. 19,000 were spent irregularly in excess of the limit prescribed under rules.

Executive Engineers Panchayati Raj (HRDF), Hissar

Rs. 39,000 were paid to Shri Bhoop Singh, S.D.O. vide Voucher No. 23 of 6.1.95 on account of temporary advance but the same has not been adjusted which resulted into temporary misappropriation of the advance amount.

Executive Engineers Panchayati Raj (HRDF), Sirsa

While taking measurements of the supply of stone, metal and Bazari, deduction @ 10 per cent and 5 per cent on account of shrinkage for voids was not made by the Engineer-in-Charge of the work which resulted into excess payment of Rs. 50,749.66 to the supplier(s).

Executive Engineers (HRDF), Thanesar

The labour engaged on daily wages was paid wages in excess of the rates of wages fixed for the monthly wage rates approved by the Deputy Commissioner from time to time which resulted into excess payment of Rs. 612471.17.

Panchayat Samiti (HRDF), Rajound

Rs. 19567.20 were paid vide Voucher No. 427 of 3/98 as labour charges on account of construction of Harijan Chopal in Village Songal but due to wrong totalling Rs. 9007.20 had been drawn in excess and misappropriated by the official concerned.

Panchayat Samiti (HRDF), Ellenabad

Muster Roll payments were made after deducting 10 per cent Contractor Profit and Service Charges instead of 21.5 per cent and thus resulted into excess payment of Rs. 11205. Table 2.2

shows the financial position as a whole of Panchayat Samities (43) audited during the year 1998-99:

Table 2.2 : Financial Position of Panchayat Samities Audited
(during the year 1998-99; in lakhs of rupees)

Opening Balance	333.53
Income	658.32
Total	991.85
Expenditure	750.60
Closing Balance	241.25

Source : Annual Report, 1998-99, Local Audit Department, Haryana.

ANALYSIS OF THE SITUATION

An analysis of the financial management by the Panchayats reveals that the funds are not being utilised and canons of financial propriety are not being followed. One of the reasons is that the elected representatives of the Panchayats are not aware of the financial rules and procedures. There is a need to organise regular training programmes in the area of audit and accounts to enable them to acquaint themselves with the financial rules and procedures.

In order to exercise a proper control over the Panchayati Raj institutions, the Government should introduce a system of internal check and inspection by its departmental officers. Government may depute any of its officers to check or inspection the accounts of Gram Panchayat, Panchayat Samiti or Zila Parishads as the case may be from time to time and to suggest changes they must make in the procedures adopted by them.

The Panchayati Raj Act and the rules framed provides for procedures to control the misutilisation of funds and the way to spend and carry out other works. However, in practice, it has been found that audit of accounts is not done regularly and a number of years lapse for want of audit. This has given rise to misuse of Panchayat funds. Moreover, the elected representatives are not aware of the financial rules and procedures, which leads to further misutilisation of funds.

The report of the Eleventh Finance Commission (EFC) is a damning indictment of the working of the Panchayats and their handling by State Governments all over the country. The EFC has come to the conclusion that the 73rd Constitution Amendment has not significantly altered the functional domain of the Panchayats at various tiers. The centrally sponsored schemes or the State level schemes for improving civic services have not been transferred to the local bodies for grassroots level planning and implementation. The EFC also found that Panchayat accounts and their audit were deplorable. The database was poor and no reliable data was available on finance, budget needs and allocations. The EFC has sanctioned Rs.1,600 crores annually for the Panchayats. It amounts to Rs. 8,000 crores for the coming five years for nearly 2.5 lakh Gram Panchayats, 6000 intermediate and 500 district level Panchayats to become the third tier of the government[10]. The distribution among the States of the financial provisions made by the EFC towards Panchayats are summarised in Table 2.3.

Based on the recommendations of the Tenth Finance Commission Rs. 82.64 crores were allocated to the Panchayats in the State for the period 1996-97 to 1999-2000, which amounts to Rs. 20.66 crores each year.

During the year 1996-97, an amount of Rs. 10.33 crores and during the year 1997-98, an amount of Rs. 15.49 crores were allocated to Zila Parishads, Panchayat Samities and Gram Panchayats as per Government of India and Haryana Government guidelines for carrying out the following works :

1. Construction of Roads.
2. Construction of Primary Health Centres.
3. Sanitation and Related Works.
4. Construction of Panchayat Bhawan and Community Centres.
5. Provision of Drinking Water.
6. Construction of Veterinary Clinics.
7. Construction of Ponds and Tanks.
8. Construction of Pedestrian Paths.
9. Arrangement of Drinking Water for Animals.
10. Provision of Irrigation Facilities on Common Lands.
11. Arrangement of Sports Facilities.

Table 2.3 : Share of States in Allocation for Panchayats

(Figures in crores of Rupees)

Sr. No.	State	Total for the State	Normal Areas	Excluded Areas	Type of the excluded areas
1.	Andhra Pradesh	9.503	8.985	0.518	Fifth Schedule Areas
2.	Arunachal Pradesh	0.348	0.348	0.000	
3.	Assam	2.918	2.814	0.104	Sixth Schedule Areas
4.	Bihar	9.813	8.721	1.092	Fifth Schedule Areas
5.	Goa	0.116	0.116	0.000	
6.	Gujarat	4.351	3.555	0.796	Fifth Schedule Areas
7.	Haryana	1.839	1.839	0.000	
8.	Himachal Pradesh	0.821	0.795	0.026	Fifth Schedule Areas
9.	J & Kashmir	0.930	0.930	0.000	
10.	Karnataka	4.926	4.926	0.000	
11.	Kerala	4.120	4.120	0.000	
12.	Madhya Pradesh	8.943	6.232	2.711	Fifth Schedule Areas
13.	Maharashtra	8.209	7.427	0.782	Fifth Schedule Areas
14.	Manipur	0.235	0.128	0.107	Hill Districts Areas
15.	Meghalaya #	0.320	0.000	0.320	Sixth Schedule Areas
16.	Mizoram #	0.098	0.075	0.023	Sixth Schedule Areas
17.	Nagaland #	0.161	0.161	0.000	
18.	Orissa	4.320	3.056	1.264	Fifth Schedule Areas
19.	Punjab	1.933	1.933	0.000	
20.	Rajasthan	6.137	5.558	0.578	Fifth Schedule Areas
21.	Sikkim	0.066	0.066	0.000	
22.	Tamil Nadu	5.826	5.826	0.000	
23.	Tripura	0.356	0.221	0.135	Sixth Schedule Areas
24.	Uttar Pradesh	16.489	16.489	0.000	
25.	West Bengal	7.222	7.222	0.000	
	Total:	100.000	87.989	12.011	

Source : Report of the Eleventh Finance Commission (2000-2005).

The entire States of Meghalaya, Mizoram and Nagaland are excluded from the provision of Part IX as per article 243 M(2).

In order to accelerate the pace of rural development and also to make the Panchayats more accountable, the Government has vested these local bodies with more administrative and financial powers. The Gram Panchayats can get works done upto Rs. 1.25 lakhs instead of 25,000 which was the earlier limit. The Panchayat Samities have been authorised to spend upto Rs. 3 lakh and the Zila Parishad can carry out works costing Rs. 5 lakhs.

As per the recommendations of the Tenth Finance Commission, the State Government during the year 1999-2000 gave a grant of Rs. 56.16 crores. The same was distributed between the Gram Panchayat, Panchayat Samiti and Zila Parishad in the ratio of 75:15:10 respectively. The funds were used for repair of roads, construction of school buildings, bylanes and paths. The Government has also decided to give cash awards to the Panchayats for their good work. The Panchayat Samities performing excellent work will be given a cash award of Rs. 5 lakh as first prize, Rs. 3 lakh as second prize and Rs. 2 lakh as third prize. Similarly, in recognition of the works of Gram Panchayats the awards will be of Rs. 50 thousand, second prize of Rs. 30 thousand and the third prize will carry a cash award of Rs. 20 thousand. These cash awards have been instituted as an incentive and recognition to encourage the Panchayats to carry out their duties effectively and efficiently.

To make the Panchayats financially viable and on the basis of the recommendations of the State Finance Commission, they have been given 3 per cent of the proceeds of stamp duty and registration fee. Similarly 20 per cent of the income from cattle fair earlier retained by the State Government has now been allocated to the Zila Parishad. The Gram Panchayats have been vested with the power to spend a minimum of Rs. 2,400 and a maximum of Rs. 8,400 on cleanliness and environment related works. For the maintenance and upkeep of the buildings of Panchayat Samities and Zila Parishads, a sum of Rs. 25 lakh has been allocated.

Financial requirements of Panchayats are being met by the State Governments Table 2.4 gives the outlay and expenditure of Panchayats Annual Plan for 2001-2002. Table 2.5 reveals the outlay and expenditure of Community Development Annual Plan for 2001-2002 and Table 2.6 shows the outlay and expenditure of Rural Development Annual Plan for the year 2001-2002. In all these plans, the Panchayats have a substantial role to play in terms of utilising the outlay.

The Panchayats are not able to keep proper accounts but they alone cannot be blamed for it. According to the Eleventh Finance Commission the Panchayats have no proper infrastructure or personnel and the States have not prepared detailed guidelines. The Local Fund Audit Director or a similar authority audits the accounts in most States. The Eleventh Finance Commission wants the audit to be entrusted to the Comptroller and Auditor General of India. Moreover, the local bodies, especially village level Panchayats, which do not have trained staff for accounts must contract out the upkeep of accounts to outside agencies. The Commission suggests a yearly grant of Rs. 4,000 for a Panchayat for upkeep of accounts.

The Commission has also pointed out that there are a number of schemes that have been taken up by the States as part of the State plans or centrally sponsored schemes for provision and improvement of civic services in rural and urban areas – such as drinking water supply, sanitation, rural roads etc. Such schemes should have been transferred to the local bodies for grassroot level planning and implementation. Transfer of such schemes to these bodies should be accompanied by transfer of funds and staff too, as in the spirit of the Constitutional amendments, and if need be, suitable legislative amendments may ensure this. Such transfer of schemes to the local bodies should, therefore, not lead to any additional expenditure liability on the state.[11]

Table 2.4 : Panchayats Annual Plan 2001-02: Outlay and Expenditure

(Rs. in lakhs)

Sr. No.	Name of the Scheme	Ninth Five Year Plan (1997-2002) Approved outlay	Annual Plan 1999-2000 Actual Expdr.	Annual Plan 2000-2001 Approved outlay	Annual Plan 2001-2002		
					Anticipated Expenditure	Proposed Outlay	of which capital content
1	2	3	4	5	6	7	8
1.	Financial Assistance to Panchayats/Panchayat Samities Under Revenue Earning Scheme	200.00	29.71	25.00	25.00	18.00	18.00
2.	Matching Grant Scheme	900.00	40.71	125.00	125.00	90.00	90.00
3.	Special Central Matching Grant to PRIs	12400.00	5681.50	2942.00	2942.00	2942.00	2942.00
	Total	**13500.00**	**5751.00**	**3092.00**	**3092.00**	**3050.00**	**3050.00**

Source : Haryana, Annual Plan 2001-2002.

Table 2.5 : Community Development Annual Plan 2001-02: Outlay and Expenditure

(Rs. in Lacs)

Sr. No.	Name of the Scheme	Ninth 5-Year Plan 1997-02	Annual Plan 1999-2000	Annual Plan 2000-2001	Annual Plan 2000-2001	Annual Plan 2001-2002	Annual Plan 2001-2002
		Outlay	Expenditure	Outlay	Anticipated Expenditure	Proposed Outlay	Capital content
1.	Construction of Chaupal (Subsidy)						
	Harijan	340.00	20.00	24.00	24.00	24.00	24.00
	Backward	70.00	5.00	8.00	8.00	10.00	10.00
	General	40.00		3.00	3.00		
2.	Construction of Office Buildings:						
	(i) Block	150.00					
	(ii) Panchayat	100.00	25.00	10.00	10.00	10.00	10.00
	(iii) Zila Parishad	145.00					
	(iv) State Panchayat Bhawan	5.00				10.00	10.00
3.	Rural Health & Sanitation Scheme	750.00	50.00	40.00	40.00	41.00	41.00
4.	Haryana Institute of Rural Development at Nilokheri (50:50).	100.00		15.00	15.00	15.00	
	Total	**1700.00**	**100.00**	**100.00**	**100.00**	**110.00**	**95.00**

Source : Haryana, Annual Plan 2001-2002.

Table 2.6 : Rural Development : Annual Plan 2001-02

(Rs. in Lacs)

Sr. No.	Name of the Scheme	Ninth Five Year Plan 1997-2002	Annual Plan 1999-2000	Annual Plan 2000-2001	Annual Plan 2000-2001	Annual Plan 2001-2002	Annual Plan 2001-2002
		Approved Outlay	Actual Expenditure	Approved Outlay	Anticipated Expenditure	Proposed Outlay	of which capital content
1.	IRDP & Allied Now SGSY (75:25) i) I.R.D.P. ii) TRYSEM Training } Now SGSY iii) TRYSEM Infra } Now SGSY iv) DWCRA } Now SGSY (75:25) v) Ganga Kalyan Yojana	4270.00 500.00 65.00 640.00 275.00					
	Total	**5750.00**	**490.85**	**385.00**	**385.00**	**300.00**	**0.00**
2.	DPAP (Now DDP) (75:25)	490.00	55.82	125.00	125.00	130.00	
3.	J.R.Y. (Now JGSY) (75:25)	3255.00	666.72	690.00	690.00	675.00	
4.	I A Y (75:25)	2500.00	427.18	400.00	400.00	425.00	
5.	M W S (75:25) (Now in SGSY)	500.00					
6.	Employment Assurance Scheme (EAS) (75:25)	9250.00	1083.77	775.00	775.00	600.00	
7.	Credit-cum-subsidy Scheme for Rural Housing (75:25)		2.93	25.00	25.00	28.30	
8.	DRDA Administration (75:25)		104.98	200.00	200.00	250.00	

Contd.

Table 2.6 *Contd.*

Sr. No.	Name of the Scheme	Ninth Five Year Plan 1997-2002	Annual Plan 1999-2000	Annual Plan 2000-2001	Annual Plan 2000-2001	Annual Plan 2001-2002	Annual Plan 2001-2002
		Approved Outlay	Actual Expenditure	Approved Outlay	Anticipated Expenditure	Proposed Outlay	of which capital content
9.	Integrated Rural Energy Programme	1230.00	95.84	100.00	100.00	120.00	
10.	Financial Assistance to assignees of the surplus land (50:50)	10.00					
	Total	**17235.00**	**2437.04**	**2315.00**	**2315.00**	**2228.30**	**0.00**
11.	PMGY (a) Rural Roads (b) Gramin Awaas			2000.00 *	2000.00	2000.00 * 251.70	
	Total	**0.00**	**0.00**	**2000.00**	**2000.00**	**2251.70**	**0.00**
12.	100% State Share Schemes Monitoring Cell	55.00	8.19	15.00	15.00	15.00	
13.	JRY Staff		257.52	325.00	325.00	305.00	
14.	DWCRA Staff		52.26	60.00	60.00	70.00	
	Total	**55.00**	**317.97**	**400.00**	**400.00**	**390.00**	**0.00**
	Grand Total	**23040.00**	**3245.85**	**5100.00**	**5100.00**	**5170.00**	**0.00**

* ACA for PMGY

Source : Haryana, Annual Plan 2001-2002.

Table 2.7 : Revenue and Expenditure of PRIs in Haryana

Revenue

(Rs. in Lacs)

ITEM	1990-91	1991-92	1992-93	1993-94	1994-95	1995-96	1996-97	1997-98
Own Tax	98	208	264	260	266	18	334	450
Own Non-tax	2841	2685	3804	3707	4006	3833	3801	4851
Own Revenue	2939	2893	4068	3967	4272	3851	4135	5301
Other Revenue	1690	1447	1521	1718	1884	2219	2796	3221
Total Revenue	4629	4340	5589	5685	6156	6070	6931	8522

Expenditure

(Rs. in Lacs)

ITEM	1990-91	1991-92	1992-93	1993-94	1994-95	1995-96	1996-97	1997-98
Expdr. on C.S.*	Nil	Nil	nil	Nil	nil	nil	Nil	nil
Other Expdr.	403.76	570.12	519.07	510.76	578.48	621.44	1649.28	2525.04
Total Expdr.	403.76	570.12	519.07	510.76	578.48	621.44	1649.28	2525.04

* C.S. = Core Services (Water Supply, Street Lighting, Sanitations and Roads).

Source : Report of the Eleventh Finance Commission, 2000-2005, July, 2000.

Table 2.8 : Revenue and Expenditure of Village Panchayats

Revenue

(Rs. in Lacs)

ITEM	1990-91	1991-92	1992-93	1993-94	1994-95	1995-96	1996-97	1997-98
Own Tax	98.00	208.00	264.00	260.00	266.00	3.00	328.00	444.00
Own Non-tax	2841.00	2685.00	3804.00	3707.00	4006.00	3833.00	3801.00	4851.00
Own Revenue	2939.00	2893.00	4068.00	3967.00	4272.00	3836.00	4129.00	5295.00
Other Revenue	1199.00	1001.00	1064.00	1214.00	1345.00	1613.00	2015.00	2449.00
Total Revenue	4138.00	3894.00	5132.00	5181.00	5617.00	5449.00	6144.00	7744.00

Expenditure

(Rs. in Lacs)

ITEM	1990-91	1991-92	1992-93	1993-94	1994-95	1995-96	1996-97	1997-98
Expdr. on C.S.*	Nil	Nil	Nil	Nil	Nil	Nil	Nil	Nil
Other Expdr.	6201.00	5288.00	8062.00	9261.00	10187.00	11484.00	8711.00	13652.00
Total Expdr.	6201.00	5288.00	8062.00	9261.00	10187.00	11484.00	8711.00	13652.00

* C.S. = Core Services (Water Supply, Street Lighting, Sanitations and Roads).

Source: Report of the Eleventh Finance Commission, 2000-2005, July, 2000.

Table 2.9 : Revenue and Expenditure of Panchayat Samities

Revenue

(Rs. in Lacs)

ITEM	1990-91	1991-92	1992-93	1993-94	1994-95	1995-96	1996-97	1997-98
Own Tax								
Own Non-tax								
Own Revenue								
Other Revenue	491.00	446.00	457.00	504.00	539.00	606.00	678.00	617.00
Total Revenue	491.00	446.00	457.00	504.00	539.00	606.00	678.00	617.00

Expenditure

(Rs. in Lacs)

ITEM	1990-91	1991-92	1992-93	1993-94	1994-95	1995-96	1996-97	1997-98
Expdr. on C.S.*								
Other Expdr.	586.00	541.00	553.80	601.00	637.80	718.40	792.10	731.90
Total Expdr.	586.00	541.00	553.80	601.00	637.80	718.40	792.10	731.90

* C.S. = Core Services (Water Supply, Street Lighting, Sanitations and Roads).

Source : Report of the Eleventh Finance Commission, 2000-2005, July, 2000.

Table 2.10 : Revenue and Expenditure of Zila Parishads

Revenue

(Rs. in Lacs)

ITEM	1990-91	1991-92	1992-93	1993-94	1994-95	1995-96	1996-97	1997-98
Own Tax						15.00	6.00	6.00
Own Non-tax						0.00	0.00	0.00
Own Revenue						15.00	6.00	6.00
Other Revenue						0.00	103.00	155.00
Total Revenue						15.00	109.00	161.00

Expenditure

(Rs. in Lacs)

ITEM	1990-91	1991-92	1992-93	1993-94	1994-95	1995-96	1996-97	1997-98
Expdr. on CS*						0.00	0.00	0.00
Other Expdr.						27.70	279.00	259.00
Total Expdr.						27.70	279.00	259.00

* C.S. = Core Services (Water Supply, Street Lighting, Sanitations and Roads).

Source : Report of the Eleventh Finance Commission, 2000-2005, July, 2000.

NOTES

1. Ranbir Singh, Haryana, in G. Ram Reddy (ed.), *Patterns of Panchayati Raj in India,* Macmillan Company of India Ltd., Madras, 1977, p. 109.
2. B.B. Misra, *District Administration and Rural Development,* Oxford University Press, New Delhi, 1983, p. 304.
3. Ranbir Singh, *op. cit,* p. 149.
4. For detailed discussion see H.D. Malvia, Village Panchayats in India, All India Congress Committee, New Delhi, 1956, p. 364-383.
5. B.S. Khanna, *Panchayati Raj in India, Rural Local Self Government,* Deep and Deep Publications, New Delhi, 1994, p. 123.
6. Government of Haryana, Haryana Panchayati Raj Act, 1994.
7. *The Tribune,* Chandigarh, Nov. 22, 2000.
8. Government of Haryana, Haryana Panchayati Raj Finance, Budget Accounts, Audits, Taxation and Work Rules, Chandigarh, 1966.
9. Government of Haryana, Annual Report, Local Audit Department, Chandigarh, 1998-99.
10. George Mathew, The Eleventh Finance Commission, *Panchayat and the Hindu,* 16.8.2000, New Delhi.
11. Report of the Eleventh Finance Commission (2000-2005), New Delhi, July, 2000.

3

CHANGING ELECTORAL PROCESSES

In a democracy, the will of the people is ascertained through periodical elections. Elections perform two important functions: they indicate the general will of the people and provide legitimacy to the government; and are a sort of referendum on the performance of the previous government. Elections are, therefore, central to modern democracies and self-governance. They are the principal mechanism for exercising control by the people on their representatives. Absence of free and fair elections also means absence of democratic functioning. Indian Constitution enjoins on the people of India to be democratic and all activities are executed within the framework of this Constitution.

The responsibility for conducting fair elections rests with the Election Commission of India. Each State has its own independent Election Commission to conduct local bodies elections. Compared to other modern democracies, India's electoral machinery is very sound and proactive. The principle of universal adult franchise is based on the principle of equity among citizens. Moreover we have the principle of "*one man one vote*" and direct election to the Lok Sabha, State Legislative Assemblies and the Panchayats. We have adopted measures to ensure the participation of the deprived sections of the society in the electoral process.

Regular, free and fair election is not only desirable but a *sine qua non* to ensure political accountability and responsiveness. Direct elections bring the voters and their representatives in direct contact. As stated earlier, the national and State level elections are conducted by an independent Election Commission. And the Panchayat level elections are conducted by the State Election

Commissions. Both have Constitutional mandate. Elections in India have acted as a catalyst of political and social mobilisation.

In a vast country like India, such a participatory journey cannot be smooth and problems are bound to be there. Indian process of political change through democratic means has, therefore, witnessed many ups and downs and many positive and negative features of electoral process have been observed. The increase in electoral malpractices and the use of money and muscle power at the national, State and local level elections is a matter of great concern and calls for urgent reforms in the electoral process. Conduct of elections in a free and fair atmosphere is a must for the survival of democracy.

PANCHAYATI RAJ ELECTIONS

Panchayati Raj has a wide sweep in so far as institution building at the local level is concerned, and so do the Panchayati Raj elections. Panchayat elections are highly significant because they bring people and local level functionaries face-to-face. Each one knows the rest and no one can fool the people by promises and unrealistic hopes. People chose their representatives to various tires of Panchayats. Panchayat level elections also provide training ground for State and national level elections. Recruitment of leaders of various socio-economic backgrounds through elections reflects the trend of social change thereby achieving the larger goal of social justice and power to the people.

The Community Development Programme launched in India soon after the Independence of the country did not click. After an euphoria of a few years, it degenerated into a bureaucratic exercise. It was felt that the involvement of the community was essential for any community development programme. The Balwantrai Mehta Committee report, discussed in the first chapter, came to the conclusion that unless people's own representatives at the local level were associated with the planning and administration of community development programmes, people's enthusiasm and co-operation would not be forthcoming to the desired extent. This led to the idea of democratic decentralisation; establishment of statutory elective local bodies; and devolution to them the necessary resources, power and authority. This helped in laying the foundation of participatory process in development programmes and thereby strengthening the democratic processes.

In the context of rural India, Panchayati Raj elections can be regarded as one of the major avenues for people's participation and social transformation. Elections also ensure a change in the outlook of the people through their own leaders; they enable them to improve their capacity to manage their affairs. One of the most important roles of elections is to discover the leadership potential in the rural people and to instill democratic values and traditions that are essential to change the feudal face of rural India.

The elections conducted in the early stages broke down the primordial loyalties and laid the path for social change and democratisation of the Indian society. However, if we look at the history of Panchayati Raj Institutions in our country and particularly that of Panchayat elections, we find that the system of local level elections could not take root and in most of the States, they were not held regularly. Due to non conduct or postponement of elections for a very long time, the Panchayats lost their relevance and came to be dominated by the bureaucracy, which suspended and superseded the remaining Panchayats at will and thereby gave a severe blow to the democratisation of rural India. The resulting *status quo* suited all the stakeholders except the deprived and marginalised sections of the society who continued to live in isolation and poverty.

Electoral Politics

In the early stages after Independence when Panchayati Raj Institutions were introduced (in 1959) and elections for these institutions were held, the local level bureaucracy helped the local elite's to capture a number of elected posts by way of their manipulative tactics. The elections were seen as a source of power and prestige. As a result in the initial stages itself, these institutions, instead of becoming the channels of popular participation, became the citadel of power politics for local influentials. As a result, the general masses were deprived of the opportunity to participate in the political process. The rural leadership that emerged was from the dominant castes and elders.

Formation of various levels of PRIs brought into open the potentials of using these institutions for ulterior purposes. As such, the MLA's, MLC's and other politicians having stake in local politics and processes, realising the strategic importance of these institutions, tried to influence the electoral process by putting up candidates favourable to them. When they did not succeed to the extent they wanted, they ensured that the Panchayats were starved of funds and other means necessary to carry out their functions. As a consequence, the PRIs failed to do much; they were superseded and re-elections were deliberately delayed.

Then there was a leadership crisis too. The newly elected representatives belonged to the dominant castes tried to corner all the benefits accruing from the system. Even though there was provision in the Panchayati Raj Acts of various States for nomination of Scheduled Castes/Scheduled Tribes and women on different Panchayati Raj bodies, the nomination process was far from satisfactory. The members from the weaker sections of the society and the women who were nominated did not participate in the meetings or the deliberations of the Panchayats and were also kept away from discharging any responsibility. Lack of education and awareness among the rural people further compounded the problem.

During the late sixties with the increase in literacy and the effects of land reforms, the elections to Panchayati Raj Institutions reflected slow but perceptible changes. The intermediatory caste was emerging stronger. Even though Panchayati Raj electoral politics revolved around the traditional factors and forces, a competitive politics was witnessed within and around the dominant castes. The strategic importance of Panchayati Raj Institutions was realised by the young, enthusiastic and educated members of the rural society. The younger elements contested a number of elections. As a result the new leadership that emerged showed a mixed trend. A sizable number of young, educated, articulate and energetic villagers also got elected to these bodies. The results of Panchayati Raj elections during these years indicated that the rural masses were getting politically conscious slowly but steadily. The value and importance of grassroots democracy was being realised even by the weaker sections of the society. This phase witnessed a perceptible change in the profile of rural leadership.

The next phase in Panchayati Raj election started in the late nineteen seventies. This period allowed political parties to put up candidates either in their formal or informal capacity, but the dominance of the upper middle level castes continued. Somehow an impression was gained that the Panchayati Raj Institutions served no purpose. Most of the State Governments treated PRIs as liabilities and elections, except in a few States, were not held. The State Governments came to exercise full control over the Panchayats.

Some Chronic Problems

The chronic problems, which adversely affected the functioning of Panchayati Raj Institutions, in almost all the States were their frequent supersession and delay in holding the elections. The Panchayati Raj Institutions depended for their survival on the whims and wishes of respective State Governments. Apart from frequent supersessions, the rules framed by the State Governments in regard to functioning of Panchayati Raj Institutions were so complex and cumbersome that it was not possible for the PRI's to adhere to them.

Despite the provisions of periodic elections in the Panchayati Raj Acts of all the States, elections were not held for 10-15 years and in some cases even for 25 years on one pretext or the other. And if the elections did take place, they were not fair. The weaker sections of the society could not contest the elections due to fear and the rural well off used their money and muscle power to win most of the seats.

This process of holding the Panchayati Raj elections further isolated the weaker sections of the society, and eroded the powers and functions of the Panchayats and the elected representatives. The Panchayats thus did not reflect the will and aspirations of the people. The vested interests destroyed the community feeling and provided further scope for people' at the helm of affairs to drain the development funds to serve their sectional and selfish ends. It may be mentioned here that the local bureaucracy fully colluded with the elected representatives in this process.

In a democratic society democratic institutions are essential. For survival of these institutions elections is important. Elections are the lifeline of democratic institutions and the lifeline of Panchayats was cut by not holding regular elections to constitute these bodies. Yet, despite all shortcomings, it was proved beyond doubt that PRI's alone can bring about the desired change in rural society. They did not function well, but they need to function well. There was no alternative to them.

IMPACT OF CONSTITUTIONAL AMENDMENT

It is in this context that the 73rd Amendment Act should be considered as an important landmark. The Act provides for an independent body to conduct elections. As per the Act, 'the superintendence, direction and control of the preparation of electoral rolls for, and the conduct of all elections to the Panchayats shall be vested in a State Election Commission consisting of a State Election Commissioner to be appointed by the Governor'. The Act also provides that if a Panchayat is dissolved before the expiry of its term of office, the elections to constitute such Panchayat for the remaining term should be held within six months of its dissolution. These two provisions in the Constitution have ensured that regular elections to the Panchayats are held.

Appointment of State Election Commission

Keeping in view the Constitutional mandate the Haryana Panchayati Raj Act, 1994*, provides that the Government shall by notification direct that a general election of Panches, Sarpanches of Gram Panchayats and Members of all Panchayat Samities and Zila Parishads shall be held by such date as may be specified by the State Election Commission.

---

* For details, see Haryana Panchayati Raj Act, 1994, specially Section 212.

The Act also provides that the Government shall constitute a State Election Commission for the superintendence, direction and control of the preparation of electoral rolls for, and the conduct of all elections to the Gram Panchayats, Panchayat Samities and Zila Parishads in the State. It stipulates that the Governor shall appoint a State Election Commissioner on the terms and conditions as may be determined by the Government. The State Election Commissioner shall not be removed from his office except on similar grounds as a judge of the High Court and the conditions of service of the State Election Commissioner shall not be varied to his disadvantage after his appointment. These features ensure the independence of the State Election Commission. The Government shall make available to the State Election Commission such staff as may be necessary for the discharge of the functions conferred on the State Election Commission.

The Act (Chapter XIX and Chapter XX) further stipulates that every Gram Sabha, Block and District shall be divided into Wards. For every electoral division there shall be a list of voters, which shall be prepared and maintained in accordance with the provisions of the Act under the superintendence, direction and control of the State Election Commission.

Registration of Voters

According to the provisions of the Act every person who is entitled to be registered as voter in the relevant part of the electoral rolls of the Assembly under the Representation of Peoples Act, 1950, shall be entitled to be registered as a voter in the list of voters for the electoral division of the Panchayat. The electoral roll of the Assembly prepared under the provisions of the Representation of People Act, 1950, for the time being in force for such part of the constituency of the Assembly will be the list of voters for that electoral division.

The civil courts have been barred from entertaining or adjudicating upon any question whether any person is or is not entitled to have his name included in the list of voters or to question the legality of any action taken or decision given by or under the authority of the State Election Commission in connection with the preparation, maintenance or revision of any such list. The Act also provides for the grounds on which an elected member of the Panchayat can be disqualified. Canvassing in or near the polling station is prohibited and penalty is prescribed for disorderly conduct in or near polling station or at the polling station.

The Act states that no person who is a returning officer or a presiding or polling officer at an election or an officer or official appointed by the State Election Commission to perform any duty in connection with an election shall in the conduct of election act for the furtherance of the prospects of the elections of a candidate. Further, any person who at any election, fraudulently takes or attempts to take a ballot paper out of a polling station or wilfully aids or abets the doing of any such act shall on conviction, be punished with imprisonment for a term which may extend to three months or with fine which may extend to five hundred rupees or both. Section 187 of the Act prescribes the nature of offences and the penalties for such offences.

Voter's list is the most crucial and sensitive parameter in the election process and it needs to be prepared according to the procedures laid down by the Haryana Panchayati Raj Rules. As per Section 163 of the Haryana Panchayati Raj Act for every electoral division, there shall be a list of voters, which shall be prepared and maintained in accordance with the provision of the Act under the superintendence, direction and control of the State Election Commission.

As per Rule 8 of the Panchayati Raj Election Rules, 1994, the Commission shall, subject to the provision of the Act, cause to prepare a Ward-wise list of voters in Devnagri/Hindi script of each Gram Panchayat, Panchayat Samiti and Zila Parishad. As per Rule 9, each voter's list prepared shall be published and affixed at the office of the Gram Panchayat, Panchayat Samiti or Zila Parishad.

The District Electoral Office shall after holding such summary enquiry into the claims or objections record his decision in writing within three days of the date of receipt of the claim and shall make available on demand copy of such decision to the objector free of charge. Rule 10(3) gives an authority to the District Electoral Officer to amend the voter's list in accordance with his decision. The voter's list so amended shall be final and a copy duly signed by the District Electoral Officer, shall be kept in his office and another copy in the office of District Election Officer (Panchayat) and shall be published in the prescribed manner. The voter's list is available to the public for inspection on payment of nominal fee, and is obtainable from the District Electoral Office. No person shall be entitled to have his name included in the voter's list for more than one electoral division of the same Gram Panchayat, Panchayat Samiti and Zila Parishad. The government shall make available to the State Election Commission such staff as may be necessary for the performance of any duty in connection with the preparation and revision of list of voters for electoral division and assist to conduct elections in respect of Gram Panchayats, Panchayat Samities and Zila Parishads.

Qualification of Contestants

Every person whose name is in the voters list, shall, unless disqualified under this Act or any other law for the time being in force, be qualified to vote at the election of a member for the electoral division to which such list pertains. Further every person who has attained the age of twenty-one years and whose name is in the list of voters, shall unless disqualified under this Act or under any other law for the time being in force, be qualified to be elected from any electoral division. No person whose name is not entered in the list of voters for the villages shall be qualified to be elected from any electoral division.

No person shall be a Sarpanch, Up-Sarpanch or a Panch of a Gram Panchayat or a member of a Panchayat Samiti or Zila Parishad or continue as such who has, whether before or after the commencement of this Act, been (a) convicted of an offence under the Protection of Civil Rights Act, 1955, (b) has been adjudged by a competent court to be of unsound mind, (c) has been adjudicated an insolvent and has not obtained his discharge, or (d) has been removed from any office held by him in a Gram Panchayat, Panchayat Samiti or Zila Parishad before the commencement of this Act, (e) has been disqualified from holding office under any provision of this Act and the period for which he was so disqualified has not elapsed, or (f) holds any salaried office or office of profit in any Gram Panchayat, Panchayat Samiti, or Zila Parishad, (g) is a servant of Government or a servant of any local authority, (h) has more than two living children, provided that a person having more than two children on or upto the expiry of one year of the commencement of this Act, shall not be deemed to be disqualified.

Two-child Norm

The Act debars pesons having more than two children from contesting any elected post. This provision was challenged in courts in at least three States. Three petitions were filed in the Andhra Pradesh High Court, challenging the Constitutional validity of Section 19(3) of the Andhra Pradesh Panchayat Raj Act, 1994, which disqualifies a person who has more than two children from holding a post in the PRI's in the State. All the three petitioners, having more than two children at the time of contesting elections, had been elected for different posts in Panchayats, but proceedings had been started for disqualifying them from holding their posts when another child was born to each of them.

Three arguments were put forward on behalf of the petitioners. First, the impugned provision violates the right to privacy of the petitioners as enshrined under Articles 19 and 21 of the Constitution. Second, it has no nexus with the purpose which is sought to be achieved through the Act *i.e.* population control. Third, the impugned provision violates Article 14 of the Constitution, which provides for equality before law, as members of Parliament and State Legislatures face no such disqualification.

The High Court examined all the three arguments in detail and came to the conclusion that the provision for a two-child norm for Panchayat representatives stood the test of law. The Court held that Section 19 (3) did not directly interfere with the right of any citizen to take a decision in the matter of procreation. It only creates a legal disability on the part of a person who has procreated more than two children to contest for or hold a public office under the Panchayati Raj Act. Moreover, the right to contest an elected office is not a fundamental right but only a legal right arising out of a statute. That being so no grievances could be made out on the ground that the right to liberty and right to privacy is taken away by the law.

Whether the restriction such as the one created in this case would in fact achieve the objective sought to be achieved or not only the future would tell, the legislative measures as such is reasonably connected with the object so sought. The court felt that it would not be justified in making a further inquiry as to what extent such a purpose would be achieved. Lastly the legislature while bringing out a particular enactment need not embrace all categories within its scope. It is for the legislature to determine the categories it wishes to embrace within the scope of the legislation. Hence the principle of equality before law was not violated by the legislation in question.

After the Panchayat elections in Haryana some complaints have been received asking the Deputy Commissioners to disqualify an elected representative on the grounds that they have more than two children. The district administration has asked the District Development and Panchayat Officers to inquire into the matter. But so far no disqualification has taken place on grounds of more than two children.

Reservations for Weaker Sections

Haryana Panchayati Raj Election Rules, Section 5(1) states that determination of reserved seats for the Wards, shall be entrusted upon respective Sub-Divisional Officer (Civil) in case of Gram Panchayat and Panchayat Samiti and Deputy Commissioner in case of Zila Parishad. For the purpose of determination of maximum population of persons belonging to Scheduled Castes and Backward Classes, the percentage of their population in each Ward shall be considered. According to Haryana Panchayati Raj Act seats shall be reserved for the Scheduled Castes in every Gram Panchayat and the number of seats so reserved shall bear, as nearly as may be the same proportion to the total number of seats to be filled by election in that Panchayat as is the population of Scheduled Castes in Panchayat area bears to the total population of that area. Such seats may be allotted to such

Wards having maximum population of persons belonging to Scheduled Caste.

It is further provided that not less than one-third of the total number of seats reserved under sub-section (1) of Section 9 shall be reserved for women belonging to the SC and such seats may be allotted by rotation and by draw of lots to different Wards. Every Panchayat shall have one Panch belonging to Backward Classes in case their population is two per cent or more of the total population of the Sabha area. Such seats shall be allotted to such Ward having maximum population belonging to Backward Classes. For the purpose of allotting Wards by lots as per Haryana Panchayati Raj Election Rules, Rule 5 (2b) the Sub-Divisional Officer or Deputy Commissioner shall publish a notice and affix it at a conspicuous place or at the headquarters of the concerned Gram Panchayat, Panchayat Samiti and Zila Parishad. The information contained on the notice aims at benefiting everybody by stating that the lots shall be drawn in the office as named in such notice and on the date and time specified therein and invite the persons to be present to witness the draw of lots. Similarly the draw of lots for seats of women belonging to Scheduled Caste shall be drawn out of the Wards reserved for Scheduled Caste category. The proceedings shall be recorded in writing and signed by the authorities. Signatures or thumb impressions of atleast two non-official persons alongwith their addresses witnessing the draw of lots shall also be obtained on such proceedings. Finally, as per the provisions of reservation and draw of lots the seats shall be allotted to specific Wards within seven days of the publication of list under Rule 4 (a) and the list of final Wards shall be duly displayed in the offices of Gram Panchayat, Panchayat Samiti and Zila Parishad.

ELECTION RULES

We find that comprehensive provisions exist in the 1994 Act, to ensure a regular, free and fair elections in the State. To conduct the elections the Haryana Panchayati Raj Election Rules were framed in 1994 in exercise of the powers conferred by sub-sections (1) and (2) of Section 209 of the Haryana Panchayati Raj Act, 1994. Chapter II, Rule 4, of the Panchayati Raj Rules states that each Panchayat area shall be divided into as many Wards as the number of seats for Panches, in such manner that the population of each Ward, as far as practicable shall be the same throughout the Gram Sabha area. Sub-Rule 2, provides that the wards in Gram Sabha area shall be demarcated keeping in view the compactness of houses on ground and similarly in the case of Wards for Panchayat Samities and Zila Parishads, these shall be demarcated keeping in view, the compactness of village on ground as far as possible. According to Sub-Rule 3, in any Ward of Panchayat Samiti or Zila Parishad the Sabha area shall be completely included as far as possible.

Adequate procedures have also been laid down for publication, verification and appeal against the order of the Circle Revenue Officer and Deputy Commissioner as the case may be. Procedure for reservation of seats in the Wards and reservation of seats for Chairperson has also been defined. Chapter IV of the Rules relates to the preparation of the voters list, its publication and the method of disposal of claims and objections (Rules 8-13), Chapter V, deals with the administrative machinery for conduct of the elections. It empowers the State Election Commissioner to issue such special or general orders of direction, which may not be inconsistent with the provisions of the Act for fair and free elections. It also provides for appointment of District Election Officer (Panchayat), Returning Officer (Panchayat), Assistant Returning Officer (Panchayat), Presiding and Polling Officers for the conduct of the elections. These persons appointed in accordance with these rules, shall within the overall direction and control of the Commission, work under the control of District Election Officer (Panchayat).

Conduct of Elections

Chapter VI of the Haryana Panchayati Raj Rules deals with the procedures regarding conduct of elections. It deals with the provisions regarding nominations, deposits, and scrutiny of nominations, withdrawal of candidates, symbols of elections and the publication of list of contesting candidates. Chapter VII deals with the appointment of election agent and revocation of such appointment. Polling and voting for election is provided in

Chapter IX that has provisions regarding the manner of voting at election and the design of the ballot box. It also provides that every ballot paper shall be of such design as may be approved by the Election Commissioner. This chapter deals with the entire process from issue of ballot papers to fresh polls in case of destruction of ballot boxes. Chapter X provides for the provisions to be followed in counting the votes to the process of declaration of results.

Thus we find that the Panchayati Raj Act of 1994 and the Haryana Panchayati Raj Rules of 1994 are very comprehensive and cover every detail and procedure to be followed so that a free and fair election can be conducted. It is under these provisions that the Panchayati Raj elections of 1994-95 and 2000 were held under the supervision of the State Election Commission. Nearly 122.78 lakh voters of about 7 lakh villages went in to elect 5958 Sarpanches and 54,181 Panches of Gram Panchayats, 2,518 members of Panchayat Samities and 303 members of Zila Parishads and in 2,000 elections 85,90,880 voters went to elect 6,019 Sarpanches, 54,345 Panches, 2,426 members of Panchayat Samiti and 314 members of Zila Parishad. The elections were held at 15,998 polling stations spread throughout the State. To understand the electoral process better we have discussed the election provisions in detail.

Arrangements for Elections

Under Section 161 (1) of the Act as soon as the notification is issued by the Government, the election of Panches, Up-Sarpanches and Sarpanches of Gram Panchayats, Members, Chairman and Vice-Chairman of Panchayat Samiti and members, President and Vice-President of Zila Parishad shall be held on such date as the State Election Commission may notify in this behalf :

- Provided that in the case of re-constitution of Gram Panchayat, Panchayat Samiti or Zila Parishad on account of the expiry of their duration of five years, such date shall not be earlier than two months or later than fifteen days before the expiry of the duration.

- The superintendence, direction and control of the conduct of such election shall be vested in the State Election Commission.

Delimitation of Electoral Wards

Formation of Wards is primarily the responsibility of the Government. Wards are made by Government officials in accordance with the guidelines provided in the Haryana Panchayati Raj Rules, 1994. It forms the essential part of the election process, but Election Commission does not have direct involvement in the formation of Wards.

The Haryana Panchayati Raj Election Rules, 1994, Section 4, states that each Panchayat area shall be divided into as many Wards as the number of seats for Panches, in such a manner that the population of each as far as practicable should be the same throughout the Sabha area. "The Ward in Sabha area shall be demarcated keeping in view the compactness of houses on ground and similarly in case of Wards for Panchayat Samities and Zila Parishads, these shall be demarcated keeping in view the compactness of villages on ground as far as possible.

Further it has been provided that every Ward shall be assigned a separate serial number of each level of Panchayat and the list of Wards determined under the rule shall be published by the Circle Revenue Officer in case of Gram Panchayat and by Deputy Commissioner in case of Panchayat Samiti and Zila Parishad. There can be an objection to this list by voters of the Sabha area, Panchayat Samiti area and Zila Parishad to which the Circle Revenue Officer (CRO) or a Sub-Divisional Officer (Civil), as the case may be, shall hold inquiry into every objection and shall record his decision within five days from the date of receipt of such objections and the list of Wards as finalised after decision of appeals shall be published by CRO and DC as the case may be.

Nomination and Scrutiny

The Haryana Panchayati Raj Election Rules provide for the procedure for the nominations of candidates. Rule 26(1) states that any person may be nominated as a candidate for election to fill a seat if he is qualified to be elected to fill that seat under the provisions of the Act. Rule 26(3) states that a nomination paper shall be supplied by the Returning Officer (Panchayat) to any voter on demand. Further, it is provided that each candidate shall in person deliver to the Returning Officer (Panchayat) or Assistant Returning Officer (Panchayat) so authorised by the Returning Officer (Panchayat) for that purpose during the time and at the place specified in the notice a duly completed nomination paper in Form 4 and signed by the candidate. It is further provided that a candidate shall not be deemed to be duly nominated for election unless he has deposited or caused to be deposited in Government treasury or sub-treasury or with the Returning Officer (Panchayat) in cash the required sum.

The Returning Officer (Panchayat) shall on receiving the nomination paper under Rule 27 inform the person or persons delivering the same, of the day, time and place fixed for the scrutiny of nomination paper and shall enter on the nomination paper its serial number and shall sign thereon a certificate stating the date on which and the hour at which the nomination paper has been delivered to him. Rule 30(1) provides that on the date fixed for the scrutiny of nomination papers under Rule 24, the candidates, their electoral agents and one other person duly authorised in writing by each candidate may attend at the time and place appointed in this behalf and the Returning Officer (Panchayat) shall give them all reasonable facilities for examining the nomination papers of all the candidates.

Sub-Rule (7) provides that immediately after all the nomination papers have been scrutinised and decisions accepting or rejecting the same have been recorded, the Returning Officer (Panchayat) shall prepare a list of candidates whose nomination papers have been accepted. After the scrutiny is over the Returning Officer (Panchayat) shall affix the list on his notice board and shall record the date on which, and the time at which, the list was so affixed. Rule 31(1) provides for the procedure for the withdrawal of candidature and Rule 32(1) provides that immediately after the expiry of the period within which candidature may be withdrawn, the Returning Officer (Panchayat) shall prepare and publish in Forms 6, 7, 8 or 9 a list of contesting candidates. The Returning Officer (Panchayat) shall after its preparation affix a list of contesting candidates alongwith symbols allotted to them on the notice board of his office and also shall supply a copy to each of the contesting candidates on demand.

Allotment of Election Symbols

The allotment of election symbol plays a significant role in the election process. The procedure of allotment of symbols to candidates for different positions in the elections and the Wards has been probed in this section. Pre-requisites pertaining to the allotment of election symbols such as appropriate timing, uniformity of procedures, variety of symbols for different Wards etc. and distribution of specimen copies of election symbols have been examined.

It is provided in Rule 33 of the Haryana Panchayati Raj Election Rules, 1994, that where a poll becomes necessary the Returning Officer (Panchayat) shall assign to each candidate any one of the symbols determined by the State Election Commissioner in the manner prescribed by him. A list of symbols shall be published by the State Election Commissioner in the official gazette and he may in the like manner add or vary any such list. The allotment by Returning Officer (Panchayat) of any symbol to a candidate shall be final and every candidate or his election agent shall be informed of the symbol allotted to the candidate.

The Haryana Panchayati Raj Election Symbols (Reservation and Allotment) Order, 1996 provides for specifications, reservation, choice and allotment of symbol at election to Panchayats in the State for the recognition of political partics. The State Election Commission shall notify from time-to-time the election or elections which shall be held on party-basis and the election or elections which shall not be held on party basis. The State Election Commission shall notify from time to time; (a) the list of reserved symbols and the list or lists of free symbols for use in an election or elections by the political party; and (b) the list or lists of free symbols for use in an election or elections by the candidates other than political parties.

The State Election Commission shall notify from time-to-time the list of recognised political parties and the symbols respectively reserved for them and the list of registered but unrecognised political parties. In every contested election, a symbol shall be allotted to a contesting candidate in accordance with the provisions of this order and different symbols shall be allotted to different contesting candidates. In an election not held on party basis, every candidate shall declare in the nomination paper first filed by him, his choice of three free symbols from the list of free symbols for that election indicating the order of his preference. The symbol shall be allotted in accordance with the procedure laid down. No candidate will ask for any other symbol but for the symbol notified by State Election Commission. In case any such symbol which is not notified by the State Election Commission is asked by any candidate the same will be ignored.

In an election not held on party basis the symbols shall be allotted to the contesting candidates for the office of Panch and Sarpanch from the list of symbols notified by the State Election Commission. This shall be in order of the list of contesting candidates prepared in 'Hindi' in alphabetical order on the last day of withdrawal of nomination, even if the contesting candidates agree among themselves upon their symbol. In an election held on party basis every candidate set up by a recognised political party shall seek the symbol reserved for that party and no other symbol and he shall be allotted the same, but no other symbol. Every candidate who is set up by a registered but unrecognised political party or who is an independent candidate shall declare in the nomination paper first filed by him, his choice of three free symbols from the list of free symbols for that election indicating the orders of his preference. The symbol shall be allotted in accordance with the procedure laid down.

If the State Election Commission is satisfied on information in its possession that a recognised political party under the provisions has failed or has refused or is refusing or has shown or is showing defiance by its conduct; (a) to observe the provisions of the 'Model Code of Conduct' for Guidance of Political parties and candidates as issued by the State Election

Commission from time-to-time; (b) to follow or carry out the lawful directions and instructions of the State Election Commission given from time-to-time with a view to furthering the conduct of free, fair and peaceful elections or safeguarding the interests of the general public and the electorate in particular, the State Election Commission may, after taking into account all the available facts and circumstances of the case and after giving the party, a reasonable opportunity of showing cause in relation to the action proposed to be taken against it, either suspend, subject to such terms as the State Election Commission may deem appropriate, or withdraw the recognition of such party for the elections.

Symbol Design and Size of Ballot Papers

The question of varieties of symbols and the designs of the ballot papers in the election process are equally important aspects. Rule 41 of the Haryana Panchayati Raj Election Rules, provides that every ballot paper shall be of such design as may be approved by the State Election Commission. However, the ballot papers for election of Panches, Sarpanches, members of Panchayat Samiti and members of Zila Parishad shall be in four different colours throughout the State of Haryana. Further, the name of the concerned candidate shall be written in Devnagri script in the ballot-paper against his/her symbol in the same order as it appears in the list of contesting candidates. On top of the back side of the ballot paper, the number of Ward and the number of polling station in case of election of Panch, the name of village and number of polling stations in case of election of Sarpanch, the number of Ward and the number of polling station in case of election of member of Panchayat Samiti and the number of polling station in case of election of member of Zila Parishad, shall be written. In order to ensure free and fair elections, under Rule 45 the following provisions have been made to discourage any attempt of tampering of the ballot boxes during the elections :

(1) The Presiding Officer at each polling station shall immediately before the commencement of the poll, allow inspection of each box, to be used at the poll, by

the candidates and their polling agents, who may be present at such station, and demonstrate to them and to all other persons present, that it is empty.

(2) The Presiding Officer after complying with the above provisions secure and seal the box in such manner that the slit in the box for insertion of ballot papers therein remains open and shall also allow the candidates or their polling agents who may be presented to affix their own seals on the space in the box meant if they so desire.

(3) The seals to be used for ballot boxes shall be affixed in such manner that it shall not be possible to open the box again without breaking such seal or any thread on which the seals have been affixed.

Counting of Votes

The process of counting of votes has been considered as another important aspect in the election process. A number of complaints arise during counting of votes. To check this a number of safeguards have been incorporated According to the Haryana Panchayati Raj Election Rules, 1994, Rule 62, every election where a poll is taken, votes shall be counted under the supervision and direction either of Returning Officer (Panchayat) or Assistant Returning Officer (Panchayat) and each contesting candidate and his counting agents shall have a right to be present at the time of counting.

As per Rule 63 (1), the Returning Officer (Panchayat) and such other officer authorised by him shall exclude from the place fixed for counting of votes all persons except :

- Such persons as he may appoint to assist him in counting,
- Persons authorised by the State Election Commissioner or District Election Officer (Panchayat),
- Public servants on duty in connection with the election,
- Candidates and their counting agents.

The Returning Officer or such other officer authorised by him in this behalf, shall decide which counting agent or agents shall watch the counting at any particular counting table or group of tables.

After the completion of the counting, the Returning Officer (Panchayat) or such other officer authorised by him shall record in the result sheet in forms mentioned in sub-rule (2) of Rule 66, the total number of votes polled for each candidate and announce the same. After the announcement of the results, a candidate or in his absence, his agent may apply in writing to Returning Officer (Panchayat) for a recount of all or any of the ballot papers already counted, stating the grounds on which he demands such recount, which he should have to mention. On such an application being made the Returning Officer (Panchayat) or the officer authorised by him shall decide the matter and may allow the application in whole or in part thereof or may reject it *in toto*, if it appears to him to be unreasonable. In this regard every decision of the Returning Officer (Panchayat) or such other officer authorised by him, under Rule (3) shall be in writing and contain the reasons therefor.

Declaration of Results

As per Rule 70 (1)(a), the Returning Officer (Panchayat) or the Assistant Returning Officer (Panchayat) shall declare to be elected the candidate for office of Panch, one who has secured the largest number of valid votes and certify the return of election in Form 18.

Similarly, the result of Sarpanch shall also be declared forthwith but if there are more than one polling station in Sabha area, the result sheets for the office of the Sarpanch shall be sent to the polling station presided over by the Presiding Officer nominated by the District Election Officer (Panchayat) on the same day and who shall, after compiling the result sheets in Form 19 declare forthwith the candidate who received the largest number of valid votes, elected as Sarpanch. For the purpose of declaration of office of Panch and Sarpanch, the Presiding Officer shall be deemed to be Returning Officer and in case of more than one polling station in the Sabha area nominated Presiding Officer shall be deemed to be the Returning Officer for declaration of results for the office of Sarpanch.

The Presiding Officer shall send the result sheet for the offices of members of Panchayat Samiti and Zila Parishad to the concerned Returning Officer for Panchayat Samiti at Block level and to the Deputy Commissioner respectively. The Returning Officer (Panchayat) or the officer authorised by them shall send the signed copy of the returns as per the rule to the District Election Officer (Panchayat) and to the State Election Commissioner.

Election Petitions

The validity of elections can be challenged in the courts. Section 176 of the Haryana Panchayati Raj Act, 1994 specifies that if the validity of any election of a member of a Gram Panchayat, Panchayat Samiti and Zila Parishad is brought in question by any person contesting the election or by any person qualified to vote at the election to which such question relates, such person may at any time within thirty days after the date of declaration of results of the election, present an election petition to the civil court having ordinary jurisdiction in the area within, which the election has been or should have been held for the determination of such questions:

A petitioner shall not join as respondent to his election petition except the following persons :

(a) Where the petitioner in addition to challenging the validity of the election of all or any of the returned candidates claims a further relief that he himself or any other candidate has been duly elected, all the contesting candidates other than the petitioner and where no such further relief is claimed, all the returned candidates;
(b) Any other candidate against whom allegations of any corrupt practices are made in the election petition.

All election petitions, received under sub-section (1) of Section 176 in which the validity of the election of members to represent the same electoral division is in question, shall be heard by the same Civil Court. Further, if on holding such inquiry the Civil Court finds that a candidate has for the purpose of election committed a corrupt practice within the meaning of sub-section (5), he shall set aside the election and declare the candidate disqualified for the purpose of election and fresh election may be held.

The Role of Government Officers

It has been observed that the Election Commission has made strenuous efforts to conduct the elections as per the provisions of the Haryana Panchayati Raj Act and the Rules framed thereafter. The Commission has further issued quite judicious instructions in providing framework, guidance and specific tasks to be performed at each and every stage of election for all officials involved in election process so that elections are conducted in a free and fair manner. The job role of the Assistant State Election Commissioner is very important. The Assistant State Election Commissioner will have the following functions to perform on on-going basis :

1. Supervise, checking and monitoring the tasks/operations being prepared by the Government staff in helping the Commission such as preparation of voters list.
2. Procure the necessary stores well in advance from the Election Commissioner.
3. Checking and monitoring the pasting of notification and all such instructions which are necessary and useful for the public participating in the election.
4. Maintaining the records and stores for all election materials such as ballot papers, ballot boxes, receipt books, cloth/ink/pad/stamps etc.
5. Training the staff in the field to be appointed for the election duty.
6. Disseminate the various instructions of the State Election Commissioner to the other field officers involved in the conduct of the elections such as Returning Officers, Presiding Officers and Polling Officers.
7. Distribution of election materials for the conduct of elections.

8. Monitoring cases of the district regarding the results declared, petitions against rejection of nominations or any other.
9. Maintaining liaison with the observers for any information required by them or helping them to perform their functions.
10. Developing liaison with the district officers in the conduct of the election.
11. Conduct Awareness Programmes to educate the voters regarding election procedures.

Returning Officers

The Returning Officer (Panchayat) plays a significant role in the conduct of the Panchayat elections. According to the Haryana Panchayati Raj Election Rules, Rule 16, the State Election Commission or when so authorised by him, the District Election Officer (Panchayat) shall appoint an officer of the Government not below the rank of Class II Officer as a Returning Officer (Panchayat) for every election to fill a seat in Panchayat Samiti or Gram Panchayat. It shall be the general duty of the Returning Officer (Panchayat) to perform all such acts as may be necessary for effectively conducting the election in the manner provided. The State Election Commissioner or if he permits, the District Election Officer (Panchayat) may appoint one or more persons as Assistant Returning Officer (Panchayat) to assist the Returning Officer (Panchayat) in the performance of his duties.

For implementation of the Act, rules for Panchayat elections have been framed accordingly. Rule 29 provides that the Returning Officer (Panchayat) shall, on receiving the nomination papers under Rule 27 inform the person or person delivering the same, of the day, time and venue fixed for the scrutiny of nomination and shall enter on the nomination papers its serial number and shall sign thereon a certificate stating the date and the hour at which nomination papers have been delivered to him.

As per Rule 30, on the date fixed for the scrutiny of the nomination papers, the candidates, their election agents and other persons duly authorised in writing by each candidate but no other person may attend at the time, place appointed in this behalf under Rule 24 and the Returning Officer (Panchayat) shall give them all reasonable facilities for examining the nomination papers of all candidates which have been delivered as required by Rule 27.

Presiding Officers

The Presiding Officers and Polling Officers shall be appointed by the Returning Officer (Panchayat) to assist in his functioning, provided that no person, who is not a government servant or a servant of any authority under the Municipal law or any public undertaking under government shall be appointed as Presiding Officer. It is further provided that if a Polling Officer is absent from the polling station, the Presiding Officer may appoint any person, who is present at the polling station other than a person who has been employed by or on behalf or has been otherwise working for a candidate in or about the elections to be the Polling Officer during the absence of the former officer and inform the Returning Officer (Panchayat) accordingly.

A Polling Officer shall subject to the direction of the State Election Commissioner, if so authorised by Presiding Officer, perform all or any of the functions of the Presiding Officer. The Presiding Officer at the polling station has to ensure that the polls are free and fair.

4

PANCHAYAT ELECTIONS – 2000

The second elections in the State to constitute the Panchayats were held in the month of March 2000. The State Election Commission made elaborate arrangements to conduct the elections in a free and fair atmosphere, which is an essential requirement in a democracy. The elections provided an opportunity for millions of rural voters to elect their representatives. A total of 85,90,880 voters cast their votes at 15,998 polling stations to elect 6,019 Sarpanches out of which 662 (11%) were elected unopposed, 54,345 Panches out of which 29,475 (54%) were elected unopposed. At the Panchayat Samiti level 2,426 Panchayat Samiti members were elected out of which 431 (18%) were elected unopposed. Similar was the case with the members of the Zila Parishad. Out of the 314 Zila Parishad members elected, 43 (14%) were elected unopposed.

Conduct of Elections

The State Election Commission issued notification of the time schedule for holding general elections to Panchayats, *i.e.* Panches and Sarpanches of Gram Panchayats and members of Panchayat Samities and Zila Parishads in three phases but later on modified the notification to hold these elections in two phases *i.e.* on 22nd March, 2000 and 29th March, 2000. But as the Board of School Education, Haryana had issued the datesheets for Senior Secondary Certificate Annual Examina-tions, March 2000 to be held from 7th March, 2000 to 29th March, 2000, the State Election Commission Haryana decided to hold the General Panchayat Elections in the State in two phases i.e. on 12th March,

2000 and 16th March, 2000 instead of on 22nd March, 2000 and 29th March, 2000 notified earlier. This was done keeping in view the fact that almost all the polling stations as notified by the Deputy Commissioners-cum-District Election Officers (Panchayat) are located in these school buildings, and it was not possible to hold Panchayat elections unless the school buildings are made available to be used as polling stations for holding these elections.

Keeping in view the above orders, the first phase of the elections were held on 12th March, 2000 (Sunday) from 8.00 a.m. to 4.00 p.m. and polling in respect of second phase was held on 16th March, 2000 (Thursday) from 8.00 a.m. to 4.00 p.m. in all the Blocks of the districts as per details given in Tables 4.1 and 4.2.

Table 4.1 : First Phase Elections

Sr. No.	Names of Blocks Where Polls were held on 12.03.2000 (I phase)	Name of Districts
1.	Ambala and Shahzadpur	Ambala
2.	Badhra, Bawani Khera, Bhiwani and Dadri-I	Bhiwani
3.	Panipat and Israna	Panipat
4.	Kalanaur and Lakhan Majra	Rohtak
5.	Jhajjar and Bahadurgarh	Jhajjar
6.	Jind, Julana and Alewa	Jind
7.	Radaur, Sadhaura and Mustafabad	Yamuna Nagar
8.	Guhla at Cheeka and Kalayat	Kaithal
9.	Fatehabad and Tohana	Fatehabad
10.	Ladwa and Thanesar	Kurukshetra
11.	Karnal, Nissing at Chirao and Assandh	Karnal
12.	Sonepat, Mundlana and Kathura	Sonepat
13.	Farukh Nagar, Sohna Pataudi and Taoru	Gurgaon
14.	Ballabhgarh, Hodel and Faridabad	Faridabad
15.	Ateli Nangal and Kanina	Mahendergarh
16.	Rewari and Khol at Rewari	Rewari
17.	Hansi-I, Hissar-I, Barwala and Narnaund	Hisar
18.	Dabwali, Baragudha and Ellanabad	Sirsa

Table 4.2 : Second Phase Elections

S. No.	Name of Blocks where Polls were held on 16.03.2000	Name of Districts
1.	Barara and Naraingarh	Ambala
2.	Kairu, Loharu, Dadri-II,Tosham and Siwani	Bhiwani
3.	Bapauli, Samalakha and Madlauda	Panipat
4.	Rohtak, Meham and Sampla	Rohtak
5.	Sahlawas, Matenhail and Beri	Jhajjar
6.	Uchana, Safidon, Pillukhera and Narwana	Jind
7.	Bilaspur, Jagadhri and Chhachhrauli	Yamuna Nagar
8.	Pundri, Kaithal and Rajound	Kaithal
9.	Bhatu Kalan, Ratia and Bhuna	Fatehabad
10.	Shahbad, Babain and Pehowa	Kurukshetra
11.	Indri, Ghraunda and Nilokheri	Karnal
12.	Rai, Kharkhoda, Ganaur and Gohana	Sonepat
13.	Gurgaon, Nuh, Nagina, Ferozpur Jhirka and Punhana	Gurgaon
14.	Hassanpur, Hathin and Palwal	Faridabad
15.	Mahendergarh, Narnaul and Nangal Chaudhry	Mahendergarh at Narnaul
16.	Bawal, Nahar and Jatusana	Rewari
17.	Hisar-II, Adampur, Agroha, Uklana and Hansi-II	Hisar
18.	Sirsa, Nathusari Chopta, Rania and Odhan	Sirsa
19.	Morni, Raipur Rani, Pinjore and Barwala	Panchkula

As discussed earlier, the State Election Commission has the responsibility of conducting the elections in a free and fair manner. The Election Commission ensures that the officers deployed in connection with the preparation, revision, and correction of the electoral rolls for and the conduct of Panchayat elections shall not be entrusted with any other duty for the period during which they are so employed and such officers and staff shall be directed to attend the meeting at the District level, as and when fixed by the State Election Commission, in connection with preparation of electoral rolls for and conduct of Panchayat elections/bye-elections. Non-compliance of the directions issued by the State Election Commission and non-attendance of the meeting by such officers and the staff shall attract criminal liabilities within the meaning of Section 185 of the Haryana Panchayati Raj Act, 1994, Section 28 of the Haryana Municipal

Corporation Act, 1994 and Section 275A of the Haryana Municipal Act, 1973 and criminal prosecution will be initiated against such defaulting officers/officials.

In accordance with the directions of the State Election Commission counting of votes for elections to Members and Sarpanches to the Gram Panchayats would start immediately after the closing of poll. Further, the counting of votes for elections to Members of Panchayat Samities and Zila Parishads would start at 8.00 A.M. on 17th March, 2000 at the places to be notified by the concerned Deputy Commissioners-cum-District Election Officers (Panchayats). To conduct the elections peacefully orderly polling was held at 15,998 polling stations, Hissar with 1,283 polling stations topped the list (Table 4.3).

Table 4.3 : District-wise Polling Stations

Sr. No.	District	Polling Station
1.	Ambala	581
2.	Bhiwani	1133
3.	Faridabad	1070
4.	Fatehabad	700
5.	Gurgaon	1113
6.	Jind	1149
7.	Jhajjar	807
8.	Kaithal	850
9.	Kurukshetra	690
10.	Karnal	943
11.	Mahendergarh	899
12.	Panchkula	273
13.	Panipat	550
14.	Rewari	699
15.	Rohtak	731
16.	Sonepat	1059
17.	Sirsa	779
18.	Hissar	1283
19.	Yamuna Nagar	689
	Total	15998

Limits on Expenditure

In order to check use of money and muscle power, it is very important to control the expenditure incurred by the contesting candidates. The Haryana Panchayati Raj Election Expenditure (Maintenance and Submission of Accounts) Order, 1996 deals with the expenditure to be incurred by the candidates. As per the notification of the State Election Commission, Haryana, the Election Commissioner has prescribed the limit on expenditure that may be incurred by the contesting candidates or his authorised election agents in connection with the elections as member of various Panchayat bodies.

It is to be observed from Table 4.4 that there has been an increase in the expenditure limit for various posts as compared to the expenditure ceiling prescribed during the 1994-95 Panchayat Elections. There has been a marked increase in the expenditure limit for the post of Member, Zila Parishad. Even though the Election Commission has prescribed these expenditure ceilings but it has been observed during the elections that the actual amount spent by various candidates including candidates for the post of Panch and Sarpanch has been much higher than the prescribed limit. There have been frequent allegations of use of money power and alcohol to influence the voters. This has been found to be a common practice in the rural areas.

Table 4.4 : Limits of Election Expenses

Sr. No.	Post	1994-95	2000
1.	Panch (Member of Gram Panchayat)	Rs. 2,000.00	3,000.00
2.	Sarpanch of Gram Panchayat	Rs. 5,000.00	8,000.00
3.	Member, Panchayat Samiti	Rs. 20,000.00	30,000.00
4.	Member, Zila Parishad	Rs. 50,000.00	75,000.00

Source : State Election Commission, Haryana.

The State Election Commissioner further directed that the account of expenditure to be incurred by the contesting candidates of various offices in Panchayat bodies will be maintained and submitted to the Deputy Commissioner-cum-District Election Officer (Panchayat) within 30 days of the declaration of the result, in the proforma to be prescribed for the purpose and the Deputy Commissioner-cum-District Election Officer (Panchayat) in turn would send the report to the Commissioner as per provisions contained in the Haryana

Panchayati Raj Election Expenditure (Maintenance and Submission of Accounts) Order, 1996.

In case a candidate fails to submit accounts of expenditure incurred by him for, elections to Panch, Sarpanch, Member Panchayat Samities/Zila Parishads, as the case may be within the prescribed time limit, the Commission shall declare him to be disqualified. Such person will be disqualified for a period of three years from the date of the order.

As regards, maintenance of accounts it is prescribed that every contesting candidate shall either by himself or by his authorised election agent, will have to keep a separate and correct account of all expenditure in connection with the election between the dates he has been nominated and date of declaration of result both dates inclusive. However, the total expenditure shall not exceed the prescribed limit.

It is further provided that no particular party or any other association, body or individual shall put up any cut-outs, hoarding, wall paintings, buntings, arches, gates, banners, flags, advertisements in newspapers etc. without the permission of general or special authority in writing by the candidates whose election is sought to be promoted or procured by such cut-outs, hoarding etc. as expenditure on all such items shall be treated as the legitimate expenditure incurred by the contesting candidates. No contesting candidate or any individual on his behalf shall put up any cut-outs, hoarding etc. without prior permission of the concerned Government authority.

In case of any violation by the contesting candidate or his authorised agent/individual to incur any expenditure in excess of the limit mentioned it would be viewed seriously and the State Election Commission shall take stringent action.

Videography of Elections

Further to preserve the purity of election process and rendering the election truly reflective of the choice of people the State Election Commission decided that in order to enable the Commission to have a faithful and accurate record of possible violations of the standing instructions of the commission and to assess the impact of its corrective measures the District Election

Officers (Panchayat) in respect of their Districts as and when directed by the State Election Commission for a particular Gram Panchayat, Panchayat Samiti and Zila Parishad shall make arrangements to record through videography critical events during the process of electioneering, including but not restricted to the period of electioneering, the day of poll, the transport and receipt of polling material, counting of votes and the declaration of results in an independent intelligent and purposeful manner. The agencies employed shall be given proper guidance as to the likely trouble spots and type of malpractices and irregularities so as to make it a meaningful exercise.

The video films thus prepared shall be viewed immediately by the District Election Officer (Panchayat) for identifying violations of the directions of the Commission committed, if any. In cases when the District Election Officer (Panchayat) is himself competent, immediate corrective action including disciplinary action against all those found guilty shall be taken and the commission informed of the same. In case of serious infringements which the District Election Officer (Panchayat) in his judgement decides to report to the Commission the concerned video tape will be forwarded to the Commission by the quickest means possible. The tapes carefully indexed and accompanied by a brief explanatory note of the infringement towards which the attention of the Commission is proposed to be invited. The explanatory note shall compulsory mention the broad details of the violations, the persons responsible for the same and action recommended.

Restriction on Use of Vehicles

The State Election Commission has observed that during the period of electioneering private vehicles are used by the candidates, their agents and supporters for casting votes within the Ward and on many occasions anti-social elements with muscle power are openly forwarded to instill a sense of fear in the minds of the voters, so that they either vote in favour of particular candidate or abstain from voting altogether. These vehicles are also used sometimes to smuggle arms and ammunitions with a view to creating disturbances during the elections. In order to curb such undesirable and illegal activities the State Election Commission has imposed restriction to hire or procure whether on payment or otherwise only two vehicles for use by a contesting candidate himself or his agents or his supporters on the day of poll during the Panchayat elections. The contesting candidates should be issued permits as per proforma prescribed by the Commission. The permit should be issued to the contesting candidates at least two days before the day of poll. The District administration shall keep a close watch on the vehicles used by person accompanying the contesting candidates and their supporters for any possible mischief, including criminal activities like carrying of illegal arms and weapons. If any of these vehicles, either of a candidate or a private owner, is found to be involved in any such act or for carting anti-social elements with a view to intimidating or creating terror in the minds of the voters, it should be the duty of the local administration to impound such vehicles and not to release them till the process of election is completed. In addition accordingly action against the owner, the occupant and the candidates who is involved in such illegal activities shall also be taken as per law. To ensure free, fair and peaceful elections, the District administration shall launch such drive for checking the vehicles immediately upon the announcement of the election and shall continue the drive till the completion of the process of elections.

Disqualifications

The Haryana Panchayati Raj Act, 1994 provides that :

(i) No person shall be a Sarpanch, Up-Sarpanch or a Panch of a Gram Panchayat or a Member of a Panchayat Samiti or Zila Parishad or continue as such who – (a) has, whether before or after the commencement of this Act, been convicted –

(ii) Of an offence under the Protection of Civil Right Act, 1955 (Act 22 of 1955) unless a period of five years as such lesser period as the Government may allow in any particular case, has elapsed since his conviction; or

(iii) Of any other offence and been sentenced to imprisonment for not less than six months, unless a period of five years or such lesser period as the Government may allow in a particular case, has elapsed since his release.

Every candidate at an election to Panch/Sarpanch/Member Panchayat Samiti and Zila Parishad is required to furnish information under Section 8 of the Representation of the People's Act, 1951, and sub-clauses (1) and (11) of Clause (a) of sub-section (1) of Section 175 of the Haryana Panchayati Raj Act, 1994 in a prescribed proforma. The copy of the proforma should be attached to each form of nomination paper supplied to an intending candidate, so that the candidate furnishes that information alongwith his nomination paper, in any case before the date and time fixed for scrutiny of nominations. Any contestant filing a false affidavit regarding criminal record would be liable for prosecution under Section 181 of the Indian Penal Code. Further any contestant who refuses to fill the prescribed proforma would be liable for prosecution under Section 178 of the Indian Penal Code.

Unanimous Elections

In the enthusiasm for providing a democratic set-up in the villages the western type of elections and their evils have been incorporated as well. The success of village Panchayat administration will depend on the enthusiasm they arouse and the feeling of oneness among the people. If there are political manoeuvrings, then this will not be possible. Local level elections and the involvement of political parties even though indirectly are based on differences, and in the village sphere everything must be done to remove these differences. To achieve this, emphasis on unanimity is essential in order that the Panchayat may be able to do its best for village upliftment. An unanimously elected Panchayat will draw all round support of the village and will achieve greater success than another rent by disputes, which linger on following electioneering. Infact the system of electioneering that we have, carries with it the seeds of destroying all chances of integration. Unanimous elections help in maintaining the principles of harmony and goodwill.

In the first elections to Panchayats in 1953 under the Punjab Panchayat Act of 1952, nearly 50 per cent of the Panches were elected unopposed in many of the districts of Punjab of which Haryana was a part. Apart from maintaining the principles of harmony it reduces social tensions and also reduces electoral expenditure. In the Panchayat elections held in 1994-95 after the Constitutional Status to Panchayats under the new Haryana Panchayati Raj Act, a total of 357 Sarpanches and Panches were elected unopposed out of which in 239 Panchayats the Sarpanch were elected unopposed and 94 Panches were elected unanimously.

In the Panchayat elections held in 2000 out of a total of 6,019 Sarpanches 662 (11%) were elected unanimously. Similarly, out of 54,345 Panches 29,475 (54%) were elected unopposed. In the case of Panchayat Samiti out of 2,426 Panchayat Samiti members 431 (18%) were elected unopposed and out of 314 members of Zila Parishad 43 of the members were elected unopposed.

It is in the interest of all concerned that this practice should be encouraged. The Government had encouraged this practice during the 1994-95 elections by announcing cash incentives for Panchayats that elected their members unanimously. Inspite of our best efforts we have not been able to get data of the cash incentives that has been given to Panchayats after 2000 elections. This is purely on the discretion of the Government. An unanimous election also saves time and expenditure of the Government. Therefore, there is a need to encourage unanimous elections by providing incentive to the Panchayats. It is reported that all the 522 voters of Kultana village in Rohtak district boycotted the elections as village elders wanted a unanimous election of their Sarpanch. The three contenders for the post also agreed to the dictates of the village elders. Therefore a fresh date for repoll was to be decided by the State Election Commission.

Violence in Elections

Even though the Panchayat elections of 2000 were, by and large, conducted in an orderly and free and fair manner, yet violence was reported from a number of places. In village Bahu Jamalpur of Rohtak district the dispute started over a person accompanying a "near blind" voter inside the polling booth. Two rival groups came out of the polling booth and clashed. They reportedly used lathis and threw stones at one another. A member of one group fired in the air to scare the rivals. The polling came to an abrupt end following the firing incidents and some miscreants poured water into the ballot boxes. As a result of this, the Deputy Commissioner ordered the suspension of polling and asked the staff to return to their headquarters.

Barring one incident in Fatehabad, the second phase of Panchayat elections passed off peacefully in Hissar and Fatehabad districts. Though the situation was tense at some places due to a keen contest, no untoward incident was reported from Panchayats which went to elections in Hissar district.

In Faridabad district the police fired in the air to dispense a mob disrupting the Panchayat poll in Alimer village in Hathin sub-division of Faridabad district. The police resorted to firing when two groups of people, indulged in violence outside the polling station and took away election material and tore papers. Even though the Panchayat elections are not contested on party basis yet we find reports of active involvement of political parties particularly in the Panchayat Samiti and Zila Parishad elections. According to *The Tribune* dated 13.3.2001 one person was injured as workers of the INLD and the BSP clashed with each other at Mehboobshahr a village in Sirsa district. During the polling for Zila Parishad election at the village, tension between the workers of the INLD and the BSP led to a clash and a BSP supported candidate was injured.

Disturbances were reported at some booths in Jhajjar district during the polling for Panchayat elections. It is alleged that some miscreants had 'stolen' and 'snatched' ballot boxes at two places. Similar incidents were reported from a number of other districts. The incidents do not point to an alarming increase or incidents of violence. Keeping in view the magnitude and spread of Panchayat elections such incidents cannot be stopped. These incidents point more to the inadequacy in the logistics for the conduct of the elections and not in the electoral procedures and rules. It can be concluded that in Haryana barring a few incidents by and large the State Election Commission has been able to ensure a free and fair Panchayat elections. This is one of the major steps towards strengthening Panchayati Raj Institutions in the State.

Table 4.5 : Number of Gram Panchayats, Wards and Voters in Haryana

Sr. No.	Districts	Gram Pancha-yats	Wards	Members of Panchayat Samities	Members of Zila Parishad	Voters
1.	Ambala	411	3097	91	13	373472
2.	Bhiwani	464	4197	173	24	623611
3.	Faridabad	336	3137	144	18	485086
4.	Fatehabad	231	2197	107	13	538427
5.	Gurgaon	512	4451	186	24	668435
6.	Hissar	309	3393	187	23	629250
7.	Jind	299	3072	157	20	546150
8.	Jhajjar	244	2408	110	15	445649
9.	Panchkula	164	1209	48	10	127198
10.	Mehendergarh	339	2886	118	15	410043
11.	Rewari	345	2765	105	13	370315
12.	Rohtak	151	1805	99	13	387887
13.	Sonepat	316	3184	163	21	591816
14.	Sirsa	319	2944	139	17	449553
15.	Yamuna Nagar	420	3180	113	14	335913
16.	Kurukshetra	364	2843	104	13	359265
17.	Kaithal	252	2425	125	17	453282
18.	Karnal	374	3379	161	19	479418
19.	Panipat	169	1773	96	12	316110
	Grand Total	6019	54345	2426	314	8590880

Table 4.6 : Number of Reserved Wards of Different Categories in Panchayat Samities

Sr. No.	Name of Districts	No. of Panch Sami-ties	No. of Panch Samiti Members	Number of Seats of Different Categories				
				General Male	General Female	SC Male	SC Female	BC
1.	Ambala	4	91	39	20	16	12	4
2.	Bhiwani	9	173	87	47	22	10	7
3.	Faridabad	6	144	73	37	15	9	10
4.	Fatehabad	5	107	46	25	21	10	5
5.	Gurgaon	9	186	98	53	16	11	8
6.	Hisar	9	187	86	50	29	13	9
7.	Jind	7	157	74	43	23	10	7
8.	Jhajjar	5	110	54	29	14	8	5
9.	Kaithal	5	125	60	30	18	12	5
10.	Karnal	6	161	76	41	25	13	6
11.	Kurukshetra	5	104	48	27	15	9	5
12.	Panchkula	4	48	23	12	5	4	4
13.	Mahendragarh	5	118	60	33	12	7	6
14.	Rewari	5	105	50	30	13	7	5
15.	Rohtak	5	99	47	26	13	8	5
16.	Sonepat	7	163	82	42	21	11	7
17.	Sirsa	7	139	59	34	27	12	7
18.	Yamunanagar	6	113	46	27	22	12	6
19.	Panipat	5	96	46	26	14	5	5
	Total	114	2426	1154	632	341	183	116

Table 4.7 : Number of Wards Reserved in Gram Panchayats

Sr. No.	Name of the Districts	No. of Gram Panchayats	Number of Wards	Categories of Wards				
				General Male	General Female	SC Male	SC Female	BC
1.	Ambala	411	3097	1181	554	657	338	367
2.	Bhiwani	464	4197	1842	1159	526	247	423
3.	Faridabad	336	3137	1387	829	396	203	322
4.	Fatehabad	231	2197	832	507	411	227	220
5.	Gurgaon	512	4451	2040	1294	471	168	478
6.	Hissar	309	3393	1442	866	515	266	304
7.	Jind	299	3072	1343	790	423	226	290
8.	Jhajjar	244	2408	1083	634	289	178	224
9.	Panchkula	164	1209	523	332	162	67	125
10.	Mahendergarh	339	2886	1264	850	346	123	303
11.	Rewari	345	2765	1171	730	387	174	303
12.	Rohtak	151	1805	828	470	233	134	140
13.	Sonepat	316	3184	1433	854	390	201	306

Sr. No.	Name of the Districts	No. of Gram Panchayats	Number of Wards	Categories of Wards				
				General Male	General Female	SC Male	SC Female	BC
14.	Sirsa	319	2944	1117	700	536	276	315
15.	Yamuna Nagar	420	3180	1079	697	655	346	403
16.	Kurukshetra	364	2843	1115	725	438	211	354
17.	Kaithal	252	2425	1015	618	358	195	239
18.	Karnal	374	3379	1387	867	503	256	366
19.	Panipat	169	1773	784	468	231	122	168
	TOTAL	6019	54435	22866	13944	7927	3958	5650

Table 4.8 : Number of Members of the Zila Parishads and Reserved Wards

Sr. No.	District	Total Members	General Male	General Female	SC Male	SC Female	BC
1.	Ambala	13	5	3	3	2	1
2.	Bhiwani	24	12	6	3	2	1
3.	Faridabad	18	9	5	2	1	1
4.	Fatehabad	13	5	3	2	2	1
5.	Gurgaon	24	13	7	2	1	1
6.	Hissar	23	11	6	3	2	1
7.	Jind	20	9	6	3	1	1
8.	Jhajjar	15	7	4	2	1	1
9.	Kaithal	17	8	4	2	2	1
10.	Karnal	19	9	5	3	1	1
11.	Kurukshetra	13	5	4	2	1	1
12.	Panchkula	10	4	3	1	1	1
13.	Mahendergarh	15	7	5	2	-	1
14.	Rewari	13	5	4	2	1	1
15.	Rohtak	13	5	4	2	1	1
16.	Sonepat	21	10	6	3	1	1
17.	Sirsa	17	7	4	3	2	1
18.	Yamuna Nagar	14	5	4	3	1	1
19.	Panipat	12	6	3	1	1	1
	Total	314	142	86	43	24	19

REFERENCES

Institute of Social Sciences, *Panchayati Raj Update,* Vol. VII, No. 6, June, 2000. New Delhi.

Haryana Panchayati Raj Act, 1994.

Haryana Panchayati Raj Rules, 1994.

Haryana Panchayati Raj Election Expenditure (Maintenance and Submission of Accounts) Order, 1996.

The Tribune, 13 March, 2000, Chandigarh.

The Tribune, 16 March, 2000, Chandigarh.

5

EMERGING LEADERSHIP

In the success of Panchayati Raj Institutions the role of leadership is very significant. Rural leadership has been an area of concern for quite some time, particularly after the Seventy Third Amendment Act. The nature and pace of development has become complex, which calls for a dynamic and result oriented leadership. The leadership must be democratic and enjoy the confidence of the people of the village. Democratisation of rural leadership has been one of the major contributions of Panchayati Raj Institutions. In the early stages one of the major criticism against the Panchayati Raj System was that, the elites had virtually taken over the system in collusion with the local bureaucracy. A number of studies reveal that the new leadership that emerged in agrarian areas as a result of various government development schemes was essentially recruited from new land owning class. A study by the Planning Commission also pointed out that most of the village Sarpanches were recruited from upper castes. Thus, the replacement of traditional leadership of zamindars by a new land owning class was a new phenomenon that emerged in rural India after Independence. The new land owing class not only emerged as an economic but also as a political and social leader in agrarian areas.

Even some of the earlier studies on rural leadership conducted by Lewis (1958)[1], Beals (1959)[2], Ernestine (1959)[3], highlighted that the foundations of rural politics in India was caste and the rural factions were based on land, family kinship and personal feuds. Infact, Lewis in a study of a village in Delhi found that the village leadership continued to be in the hands of the Jats, the traditional dominant caste. He also observed that though status and prestige of caste leaders and their followers was declining any transfer of leadership was resisted and younger leaders were fewer. Mehta (1972)[4], studied a village in Ropar district where aged, more educated and economically well off leaders were found. D.S. Chaudhary's (1981)[5] *Study of Emerging Rural Leadership in Rajasthan* found that there was an appreciable change in the traditional pattern of rural leadership after the introduction of Panchayati Raj. Even though younger leadership was emerging it needs much more qualitative improvement. The socio-economic outlooks and attitudes of the leaders shows great signs of an appreciation for modernisation. Hargian Singh's (1985)[6] study of *Panchayati Raj Leadership in Haryana* reveals that the leadership came from smaller families yet belonged to the higher and dominating castes and was drawn from the educated segment of the society. The leadership generally had higher economic status and came mainly from agriculturists having large land holdings. It concluded that caste continued to be a relevant factor in determining the rural leadership. Prem Prashant *et al.* (1996)[7] reveals that the traditional leadership pattern was being replaced as a result of the 73rd Amendment Act. A large number of Panchayati Raj leaders were younger and belonged to the weaker sections of the society with low level of education hailing from agricultural families and generally having small land holding and low annual income. Thus, it is clear that earlier models of Panchayati Raj failed to benefit the weaker sections of the rural society. The elites emerging from higher income and more educated sections of rural society played a dominant role in the Panchayats.

It is in this context that the study of rural leadership assumes significance, especially after the introduction of 73rd Amendment Act. In the coming years these new leaders are going to play a major role in shaping the Panchayats. It is through this leadership that all the developmental works at the local level are to be carried out. It is expected that these leaders will try to engineer profound social and economic improvements by injecting new ideas, innovations, norms and values. Political development and the growth of these democratic institutions to a large extent depends on the quality of local leadership, its socio-economic background and style of functioning. On the other hand, the success of Panchayati Raj Institutions itself would depend largely upon the quality and competence of leadership available at the local level. Therefore, it is important to study these grassroot leaders who have acquired power through democratically elected bodies and who are going to be actively involved in eliciting people's co-operation in the implementation of programmes and plans relating to socio-economic development of the rural areas. The Panchayats after the 73rd Constitutional Amendment Act have come to enjoy a special status in the scheme of governance. Development of rural areas, will depend on the leadership and its capacity and capability to meet new challenges. Moreover the success and future of Panchayati Raj Institutions will to a large extent depend upon the quality and competence of leadership available at the local level. Therefore, it is imperative to know the pattern of emerging rural leadership to understand the potential thrust of these bodies.

METHODOLOGY OF THE STUDY

The focus of the study is on rural leaders who are members of the Village, Block and Zila Panchayat. As the members of the Panchayats are the subject of our study by virtue of the position they are occupying, leader identification has not been a problem. The focus is on the type of leadership that has emerged in the rural local bodies as a result of the Panchayat elections held in 2000. We will be looking mainly at the socio-economic profile of these elected representatives. This is the second Panchayat elections held in the State after the implementation of the 73rd Amendment Act. The first election to constitute the Panchayats in the State were held in 1994-95. The data has been collected from the State Election Commission, Haryana, District and Block Development and Panchayat Offices from various districts and other sources. Data pertains to 25,063 elected members at Gram Panchayats and 614 members from Panchayat Samities and Zila Parishads of 10 districts, 50 Blocks and 2,500 Panchayats in the State.

The data has been tabulated and presented category-wise. The first category deals with the data of 25,063 elected members of the Gram Panchayats. The second category consists of Sarpanches of 1,057 Panchayats. The third analysis comprises of women Sarpanches of 560 Panchayats and the fourth category of analysis is that of 614 members from various Panchayat Samities and Zila Parishads. The classification is purposive so as to highlight the salient aspects of the emerging rural leadership in the State at various tiers of local governance.

GRAM PANCHAYATS

Socio-economic Profile of Elected Members

The Panchayat elections held in 2000 have brought about a change in the composition and character of the Panchayats. Reservation of seats in favour of women has enabled them to come forward and play a role, in decision-making. Before 73rd Amendment Act, 1992 in most States women's representation in Panchayati Raj Institutions was minimal. They were a male dominated institution. But now this phenomenon has undergone a change. Table 5.1 gives the sex composition of the 25,063 elected members of Gram Panchayats. The table reveals that 66.73 per cent of the members are males and 33.27 per cent are females.

Table 5.1 : Sex Composition of Members of Gram Panchayats

Sex	Frequency	Percentage
Male	16725	66.73
Female	8338	33.27
Total	25063	100.00

Caste Composition

The problem with earlier Panchayats was that they were generally dominated by the members of the high castes. Even today caste plays a major role in rural areas. It is a factor that cannot be ignored. It has also been observed that during the elections caste affiliations play a significant role. Table 5.2 presents the caste composition of the elected members of the Gram Panchayats. It is evident that 71.63 per cent of them are from general castes, 19.11 from the Scheduled Castes and 9.26

per cent from the Backward Castes. Haryana has lesser percentage of Scheduled Castes and Backward Castes.

Table 5.2 : Caste Composition of Members of Gram Panchayats

Caste	Frequency	Percentage
General	17953	71.63
S.C's	4789	19.11
B.C.'s	2321	9.26
Total	25063	100.00

Reservation of seats is in proportion to their population. Now we find that nearly 30 per cent of the Panchayat elected representatives belong to the deprived sections of the society. This representation will enable them to have a greater role in Panchayati Raj Institutions.

Age

In the early days after Independence, the traditional village leadership was in the hands of the elders of the village. But with the increase in awareness and also due to democratic traditions reaching to the village level there is a perceptible shift in the age composition of the rural leadership.

The age classification of the elected members of the Panchayat is presented in Table 5.3. It is evident that 21.06 per cent of the representatives are from the age group of 21-30 years, while 33.88 per cent are in the age group of 31-40 years. Almost 55 per cent of the elected representatives are in the age group of 21-40 years. Further, we see that more than 75 per cent of them are between the age group of 18-50 years. The elders group of above 61 years constitutes only 11.52 per cent of the elected representatives. Thus, it indicates that more and more younger leaders are entering the Panchayats now.

Table 5.3 : Age Classification of Members of Gram Panchayats

Age Group	Frequency	Percentage
21-30 years	4715	21.06
31-40 years	7584	33.88
41-50 years	5477	24.47
51-60 years	2030	9.07
61 and above	2578	11.52
Total	25063	100.00

Educational Status

In terms of education, the finding is not very encouraging. Rural development is a very complex task and needs to be understood in proper perspective. Education helps in understanding the complexities of such problems. Moreover, it helps in building opinion and attitude. One cannot deny the fact that an educated and aware leadership is the need of the day. It will not only help in understanding the programmes and schemes but will also help in its effective implementation. The education level of the elected members of the Panchayats is revealed in Table 5.4. It is seen that 40.94 per cent of the elected representatives have had no formal schooling at all. Most of them cannot even read and write. Women members belonging to the Scheduled Castes even do not know where to put their thumb impression. Due to this they become pawns in the hands of the Panchayats and the local level bureaucracy.

Table 5.4 : Educational Level of Members of Gram Panchayats

Education Level	Frequency	Percentage
No Schooling	10262	40.94
Primary	4598	18.34
Middle	4388	17.51
Matric	4949	19.75
Senior Secondary	415	1.65
Graduation	382	1.52
Post Graduate	56	0.22
Others	13	0.05
Total	25063	100.00

Table 5.4 further reveals that only 18.34 per cent of them have studied upto primary level, 17.51 per cent upto middle school level and 19.75 per cent have studied upto Matric. Only 1.52 per cent of them are graduates and 0.22 per cent are post-graduates. An overall picture shows that more than 75 per cent of the elected members of the Gram Panchayats have studied only upto middle school. It is important that educational facilities are made more accessible in the rural areas so that women can play a meaningful role in the society.

Occupational Background

Agriculture forms the backbone of the States' economy. Therefore, it is clear that most of the elected members own land and are agriculturists. This fact is evident from Table 5.5, which shows the occupational classification of the Panchayat members. 61.24 per cent of them have agriculture as their main occupation and 11.13 per cent have no occupation. Quite a large section of the elected members (23.95 per cent) are labourers or wage workers. Most of them constitute agricultural labourers. Only 1.68 per cent of them are self-employed and 1.76 per cent are petty businessmen.

Table 5.5 : Occupation of Members of Gram Panchayats

Occupation	Frequency	Percentage
No occupation	2790	11.13
Agriculture	15349	61.24
Labourer/Wage Worker	6004	23.95
Self-Employed	422	1.68
Business	442	1.76
Others	56	0.22
Total	25063	100.00

Family Size

A look at the family size of the elected representatives reveals an interesting pattern as is evident from Table 5.6. The data of family size has been collected from six Blocks of Gurgaon district. It constitutes a total of 3,232 elected members of the Gram Panchayats. As per rules those having more than two children are barred from contesting elections with effect from 1995. Only 16.52 per cent of the elected members have two children. Table 5.6 further shows that 73.44 per cent of them have between three to eight children and 1.75 per cent have between nine to twelve children. One of the factors for having more number of children relates to the preference for a male child which have taken a serious turn as revealed in the provisional census data, which shows a decline in female ratio in Haryana. It is a good decision of the State Government to debar from elections those who have more than two children even though this decision has been challenged in the Supreme Court of India.

Table 5.6 : Family Size of Members of Gram Panchayats

(No. of children)

No. of children	Frequency	Percentage
No issue	133	4.11
1 child	134	4.15
2 children	534	16.52
3-4 children	1319	40.81
5-6 children	787	24.35
7-8 children	268	8.29
9-10 children	52	1.60
10-12 children	5	0.15
Total	3232	100.00

Income

The annual income of 644 elected representatives of the Gram Panchayats is shown in Table 5.7. They belong to Punhana Block of Gurgaon district. The annual income of the elected leaders appears to be quite low. The larger proportion of the leaders (41.30 %) have income between 5,001-10,000 rupees while 39.23 per cent have annual income between 10,000 to 15,000. On the upper side we find that 0.93 per cent of the leaders have income above 50,001 rupees.

Table 5.7 : Annual Income of Members of Gram Panchayats

(Block Punhana, Gurgaon district)

Income (in Rs.)	Frequency	Percentage
Upto 5,000	4	0.62
5001-10,000	266	41.30
10,001-15,000	253	39.28
15,001-20,000	67	10.40
20,001-25,000	33	5.12
25,001-30,000	10	1.55
30,001-40,000	4	0.62
40,001-50,000	1	0.15
50,001 and above	6	0.93
	644	100.00

Even though it is difficult to obtain reliable income data we can conclude that most of the leaders belong to the lower income strata. This can also be due to large number of seats being reserved in favour of women, Scheduled Castes and Backward Castes. Most of the leaders from this category in the rural areas will naturally belong to the lower income strata. The income profile also reveals that there is a perceptible change. Earlier the rural leadership was from higher income group which had inherent advantages.

Socio-economic Profile of Sarpanches

The Sarpanch is the elected head of the Gram Panchayat and has a major role in planning for the development of the village. He is directly elected and, therefore, represents the entire village. Under the Haryana Panchayati Raj Act, 1994, the Sarpanch has been vested with a number of powers and functions. The Sarpanch can make or unmake a Panchayat. If the Sarpanch is active, educated and aware of his responsibilities he can provide a better and effective leadership. The socio-economic profile of 1057 Sarpanches belonging to as many Panchayats has been analysed, which reveals a very interesting pattern.

Sex Composition

The data on sex composition of the Sarpanches in Tables 5.5 to 5.8 shows that out of 1,057 Sarpanches, 700 (66.22 per cent) are male and 33.78 per cent are female Sarpanches. There are a number of seats reserved in favour of women for the post of Sarpanches and that is why their participation is almost one-third. This has enhanced the participation of women in Panchayats to a large extent.

Table 5.8 : Sex Composition of Sarpanches

Sex	Frequency	Percentage
Male	700	66.22
Female	357	33.78
Total	1057	100.00

Caste Composition

As explained earlier caste plays a major role in rural politics. Table 5.9 reveals the caste composition of the Sarpanches, it is evident that nearly 80 per cent of the Sarpanches are from the

General Castes and only 20.06 per cent belong to the Scheduled Castes.

Table 5.9 : Caste Composition of Sarpanches

Caste	Frequency	Percentage
General	845	79.94
S.C.	212	20.06
B.C.	-	-
Total	1057	100.00

It is to be noted that out of the 1,057 Panchayats not even a single Sarpanch belongs to the Backward Caste. Perhaps this is because the Backward Castes in Haryana constitute a small population and no post of Sarpanch is reserved in favour of Backward Caste.

Age

The age composition as evident from Table 5.10 shows that 44.18 per cent of the Sarpanches are below the age of 40 years. It reveals that many of the Sarpanches are young and have replaced the traditional leadership. 28.95 per cent are in the age groups of 41-50 years.

Table 5.10 : Age Composition of Sarpanches

Age (in years)	Frequency	Percentage
21-30	137	12.96
31-40	330	31.22
41-50	306	28.95
51-60	179	16.93
61 and above	105	9.93
Total	1057	100.00

When we compare the age composition of the elected Panchayat members with that of the Sarpanches we find that people tend to prefer Sarpanches from the age group of 41-50 years. 28.95 per cent of the Sarpanches belong to this category while we find that nearly 26.86 per cent of the elected Panchayat members are from the age group of 51 years and above.

Education

Table 5.11 which deals with the educational level of the Sarpanches shows that 29.61 per cent of the Sarpanches have no formal schooling, while 17.69 per cent have studied upto primary school level and 14.76 per cent upto middle school level. At the Matric level the percentage is much higher (27.05%). When we compare this with the educational level of the elected Panchayat members we find that 37.92 per cent of the Sarpanches have studied beyond Matric and higher while only 23.19 per cent of the Gram Panchayat members have acquired education beyond Matric. We can conclude that generally those aspiring to become Sarpanches have better educational qualifications than those aspiring to become members of the Gram Panchayat.

Table 5.11 : Educational Background of Sarpanches

Educational Level	Frequency	Percentage
No schooling	313	29.61
Primary	187	17.69
Middle	156	14.76
Matric	286	27.05
Senior Secondary	37	3.50
Graduate	62	5.86
Post-Graduate	16	1.51
Others	-	-
Total	1057	100.00

Occupation

Most of the Sarpanches are agriculturists as revealed in Table 5.12. 73.23 per cent are land owners while 13.81 per cent comprise labourer/wage earners. An important factor is that many of the representatives in this category belong to the deprived sections of the society who have made it to the post of Sarpanch. They do not have much resource base. While 23.95 per cent of the Gram Panchayat members comprised of labourer/wage earners, only 13.81 per cent of the Sarpanches fall under this category. On the other hand, 2.93 per cent are self-employed and 2.17 per cent are petty businessmen.

Table 5.12 : Occupational Background of Sarpanches

Occupation	Frequency	Percentage
No Occupation	83	7.85
Agriculture	774	73.23
Labourer/Wage Earner	146	13.81
Self-employed	31	2.93
Business	23	2.17
Others	–	–
Total	1057	100.00

Family Size

The family size of the Sarpanches is presented in Table 5.13 which reveals that 39.41 per cent of the Sarpanches have between 3-4 children. While 22.94 per cent Sarpanches have between 5-6 children. The data pertains to 340 Sarpanches from various districts.

Table 5.13 : Family Size of Sarpanches

No. of Children	Frequency	Percentage
No Issue	7	2.06
1 Child	17	5.00
2 Children	52	15.29
3-4 Children	134	39.41
5-6 Children	78	22.94
7-8 Children	39	11.47
9-10 Children	8	2.35
11-12 Children	5	1.47
Total	340	100.00

The table further reveals that 18.29 per cent of the Sarpanches have more than seven children out of which 1.47 per cent have between 11-12 children.

Socio-Economic Profile of Women Sarpanches

Further segregating the data the focus is on women Sarpanches. Since the introduction of the 73rd Amendment Act due to reservation of seats in favour of women a large number of women have come to occupy the post of Sarpanches. The data pertains to seven districts, namely, Rewari, Rohtak, Bhiwani, Mahendergarh, Faridabad, Sonepat and Panipat. As per discussions with the officials/non-officials it was revealed that women candidates showed more interest for the post of Sarpanch, than that of a Panch. A number of women contested even against unreserved seats. Those women who had completed their term as Sarpanches contested again and in some cases were elected as well. However, during interactions in the field it was revealed that the male candidates did not like the presence of women candidates for unreserved seats and in a number of cases they were forced to withdraw.

Age

The age distribution of the women Sarpanches is presented in Table 5.14 which indicates that 11.80 per cent of them are from 21-30 age group. 33.20 per cent are from 31-40 years of age while 31.40 per cent belong to the category of 41-50 years. The pattern of age composition is similar to that of male Sarpanches. 23.60 per cent of the women Sarpanches are above 51 years of age.

Table 5.14 : Age Composition of Women Sarpanches

Age (in years)	Frequency	Percentage
21-30 years	59	11.80
31-40	166	33.20
41-50	157	31.40
51-60	66	13.20
61 & above	52	10.40
Total:	500	100.00

Education

Women in the rural areas continue to be denied access to education. This is revealed from Table 5.15 which presents the educational level of the newly elected women Sarpanches. The table shows a depressing picture of women Sarpanches educational background. 54.82 per cent have had no formal schooling. While in the case of male Sarpanches this category consisted of 29.61 per cent. Similarly 21.43 per cent have studied upto primary school level, 10.18 per cent upto middle and 10.89 per cent upto Matric. 1.61 per cent of them are graduates, and they belong to the affluent sections of the rural population who have been elected mainly from general seats reserved in favour of women. Overall 42.50 per cent of the women Sarpanches have studied between primary to Matric level while men Sarpanches constitute 59.50 per cent in this category. There is a need to focus on women's education in rural areas.

Table 5.15 : Educational Level of Women Sarpanches

Educational Level	Frequency	Percentage
No schooling	307	54.82
Primary	120	21.43
Middle	57	10.18
Matric	61	10.89
Senior Secondary	6	1.07
Graduation	9	1.61
Post-Graduate	-	-
Others	-	-
Total	560	100.00

Family Size

Medium size family appears to be the emerging pattern in the rural areas as evident from Table 5.16 which presents the family size pattern of women Sarpanches. The table shows that 17.27 percent of them have two children. 42.73 per cent have 3-4 children and 20 per cent have 5-6 children while 11.82 per cent have 7-8 children. 4.55 per cent of the women Sarpanches have more than 8 children. When we look at the data of women Sarpanches, it reveals that most of them are from the middle age group with low level of education having medium size family pattern.

Table 5.16 : Family Size of Women Sarpanches

No. of Children	Frequency	Percentage
No issue	2	1.82
1 Child	2	1.82
2 Children	19	17.27
3-4 Children	47	42.73
5-6 Children	22	20.00
7-8 Children	13	11.82
8-10 Children	2	1.82
11-12 Children	3	2.73
Total	110	100.00

Socio-economic Profile of Members of Panchayat Samiti and Zila Parishad

Haryana has a three-tier structure of Panchayati Raj System. The Panchayat Samiti (PS) is at the Block level and the Zila Parishad (ZP) at the district. The data collected and compiled pertains to 634 members of the Panchayat Samiti and Zila Parishad of which 83 are members of the Zila Parishad and 551 are members of the Panchayat Samiti from various districts. Table 5.17 reveals the position profile of the members of the higher tiers of Panchayats in the State.

Table 5.17 : Position Profile of Members of PS and ZP

Level	Frequency	Percentage
Zila Parishad	83	13.09
Panchayat Samiti	551	86.90
Total	634	100.00

Out of the total 13.09 per cent are members of the Zila Parishad and 86.90 per cent are members of the Panchayat Samiti.

Sex Composition

The sex composition of the representatives as presented in Table 5.18 shows that 65.61 per cent of them are male members and 34.39 are female members.

Table 5.18 : Sex Composition of PS and ZP Members

Sex	Frequency	Percentage
Male	416	65.61
Female	218	34.39
Total	634	100.00

Caste

Table 5.19 indicates the caste composition of the members of the Panchayat Samiti/Zila Parishad. As per Table 5.19, 75.08 per cent of them are from the general category and 19.72 per cent belong to Scheduled Castes. Backward Castes form a small segment of 5.20 per cent of the elected members in the higher tiers of Panchayat.

Table 5.19 : Caste Composition of PS and ZP Members

Caste	Frequency	Percentage
General	476	75.08
SCs	125	19.72
BCs	33	5.20
Total	634	100.00

Age

The age classification reveals that the leadership in the higher tier Panchayats is comparatively younger in age than that of the Gram Panchayat. Table 5.20 gives the age classification of the representatives of the upper tiers. From the table, it is revealed that 26.49 per cent of them are in 21-30 years age group, 40 per cent belong to 31-40 years age category and 23.86 per cent are in the 41-50 years age group.

Table 5.20 : Age Group to which P.S. and Z.P. Members belong

Age Group (in years)	Frequency	Percentage
21-30	151	26.49
31-40	228	40.00
41-50	136	23.86
51-60	42	7.37
61 and above	13	2.28
Total	570	100.00

A comparative study of the age classification of the members of the Panchayat Samiti/Zila Parishad and that of the Sarpanch reveals a number of interesting observations. Firstly, in the case of Sarpanches 44.18 per cent of them are in the age group of 21-40 years. On the other hand in the case of Panchayat Samiti and Zila Parishad we find that a very high percentage of 66.49 are in the category of 21-40 years. It shows that younger people are inclined to contest as members of the upper Panchayats as people in the villages prefer to have a more experienced person as the Sarpanch. Secondly, comparing the data of representatives who are between the age group of 51 and above years, it reveals that 26.86 per cent of the Sarpanches are from this age group while only 9.65 per cent of the members of the higher tier Panchayats form this age category. It could also be concluded that at the Panchayat Samiti/Zila Parishad level the members are less experienced when compared to that at the level of Sarpanch in the Gram Panchayat.

Education

The members of the Panchayat Samiti/Zila Parishad have a better educational profile than their counterparts in the Gram Panchayat. Table 5.21 presents the educational profile of the elected members of the upper tier Panchayats.

The level of education among the members is quite distributive unlike in the case of women Sarpanches where 54.82 per cent had not been to the school at all. In this case only 18.30 per cent of the members had not been to the school. 13.09 per cent had studied up to primary level, 13.4 per cent up to middle level and 39.75 per cent had attained education up to Matric level. 7.10 per cent of the representatives are graduates and 2.52 per cent are post-graduates. The members of the upper tier Panchayats have higher educational level than that of the Gram Panchayat leadership. 66.25 per cent of the members have educational level ranging from primary school to Matric.

Table 5.21 : Educational Level of PS and ZP Members

Educational Level	Frequency	Percentage
No schooling	116	18.30
Primary	83	13.09
Middle	85	13.41
Matric	252	39.75
Senior Secondary	32	5.05
Graduation	45	7.10
Post-Graduate	16	2.52
Others	5	0.79
Total	634	100.00

Occupation

The occupational classification of the members of the upper tier as presented in Table 5.22 shows that agriculture is the main occupation and the backbone of rural Haryana and as such 56.51 per cent of them are agriculturists. Labourer/wage workers constitute the next significant category comprising of 17.42 per cent. While 4.07 per cent are self-employed and 5.37 per cent are involved in a variety of businesses.

Table 5.22 : Occupational Background of Members of PS and ZP

Occupation	Frequency	Percentage
No occupation	98	15.96
Agriculture	347	56.51
Labourer/Wage Worker	107	17.42
Self-employed	25	4.07
Business	33	5.37
Others	4	0.65
Total	614	100.00

For a comprehensive picture we have presented the district-wise categorisation of the members of the Gram Panchayat in Tables 5.23 to 5.27. The district-wise variations can be seen from the tables.

To sum up the analysis of the socio-economic profile of the elected representatives, reveals the following pattern :

1. The members of the Gram Panchayats are mostly agriculturists, young in age with low educational level.
2. People prefer to elect Sarpanches with some level of maturity.
3. Education level among the women Sarpanches is very low.
4. Most of the Sarpanches are from the middle age group.
5. Medium size family structure appears to be the norm in the Panchayats.
6. The age composition of the members of the Panchayat Samiti/Zila Parishad is relatively younger to that of the Sarpanches.
7. The members of the Panchayat Samiti/Zila Parishad are more educated than the members of the Gram Panchayats.
8. The composition of self-employed and businessmen in the upper tier Panchayats is higher than that of the Gram Panchayats.

The above analysis also reveals that there is a need to educate and develop the capacity and capability of the elected representatives. Training must be imparted to all of them to enable them to function as per the provisions of the Act. They need to be made aware of their rights and duties. Mere transfer of powers will not be sufficient if the members are not able to exercise these powers.

Table 5.23 : Panchayats : Sex Composition

Sex	Bhiwani	Faridabad	Gurgaon	Jind	Mahindra-Garh	Panipat	Rewari	Rohtak	Sirsa	Sonepat	Haryana
Male	2801 (67.22)	1775 (64.97)	2907 (67.21)	1719 (66.91)	779 (65.79)	971 (65.60)	2013 (67.10)	1195 (66.83)	571 (67.33)	1994 (67.14)	16725 (66.73)
Female	1366 (32.78)	957 (35.03)	1418 (32.79)	850 (33.09)	405 (34.21)	509 (34.39)	987 (32.90)	593 (33.17)	1277 (32.66)	976 (32.86)	8338 (33.27)
Total	4167 (100.00)	2732 (100.00)	4325 (100.00)	2569 (100.00)	1184 (100.00)	1480 (100.00)	3000 (100.00)	1788 (100.00)	848 (100.00)	2970 (100.00)	25063 (100.00)

Table 5.24 : Elected Representatives : Age Composition

Age (in years)	Bhiwani	Faridabad	Gurgaon	Jind	Mahindra-garh	Panipat	Rewari	Rohtak	Sirsa	Sonepat	Haryana
21-30	925 (22.20)	581 (21.27)	250 (15.19)	524 (20.40)	254 (21.45)	358 (24.19)	511 (17.03)	494 (27.83)	120 (14.15)	698 (23.50)	4715 (21.06)
31-40	1427 (34.24)	977 (35.76)	455 (27.64)	906 (35.27)	337 (28.46)	557 (37.64)	978 (32.60)	602 (33.67)	305 (35.97)	1040 (35.02)	7584 (33.88)
41-50	1011 (24.27)	663 (24.27)	488 (29.65)	609 (23.70)	284 (23.97)	374 (25.27)	774 (25.80)	375 (20.97)	241 (28.42)	658 (22.15)	5477 (24.47)
51-60	495 (11.88)	305 (11.16)	230 (13.97)	347 (13.51)	200 (16.89)	122 (8.24)	457 (15.23)	187 (10.46)	116 (13.68)	332 (11.18)	2030 (9.07)
61 and above	309 (7.41)	206 (7.54)	223 (13.55)	183 (7.15)	109 (9.21)	69 (4.66)	280 (9.33)	130 (7.27)	66 (7.78)	242 (8.15)	2578 (11.52)
Total	4167 (100.00)	2732 (100.00)	1646 (100.00)	2569 (100.00)	1184 (100.00)	1480 (100.00)	3000 (100.00)	1788 (100.00)	848 (100.00)	2970 (100.00)	22384 (100.00)

Table 5.25 : Elected Representatives : Caste Composition

Caste	Bhiwani	Faridabad	Gurgaon	Jind	Mahindra-garh	Panipat	Rewari	Rohtak	Sirsa	Sonepat	Haryana
General	2981 (71.54)	1983 (72.58)	3180 (73.53)	1816 (70.69)	860 (72.63)	1050 (70.94)	2102 (70.06)	1295 (72.43)	531 (62.62)	2155 (72.56)	17953 (71.63)
Scheduled Caste	829 (19.89)	505 (18.48)	671 (15.51)	530 (20.63)	207 (17.48)	302 (20.40)	606 (20.20)	364 (20.36)	236 (27.83)	539 (18.15)	4789 (19.11)
Backward Caste	357 (8.57)	244 (8.93)	474 (10.96)	223 (8.68)	117 (9.88)	128 (8.65)	292 (9.73)	129 (7.21)	81 (9.55)	276 (9.29)	2321 (9.26)
Total	4167 (100.00)	2732 (100.00)	4325 (100.00)	2569 (100.00)	1184 (100.00)	1480 (100.00)	3000 (100.00)	1788 (100.00)	848 (100.00)	2970 (100.00)	25063 (100.00)

Table 5.26 : Elected Representatives : Educational Profile

Education	Bhiwani	Faridabad	Gurgaon	Jind	Mahendragarh	Panipat	Rewari	Rohtak	Sirsa	Sonepat	Haryana
No Schooling	1633 (39.18)	1121 (40.03)	2113 (61.79)	1280 (49.82)	492 (41.55)	567 (38.31)	957 (31.90)	540 (30.12)	517 (60.97)	1042 (35.08)	10262 (40.94)
Primary	750 (18.00)	731 (26.76)	763 (17.64)	366 (14.25)	144 (12.16)	286 (19.32)	543 (18.10)	362 (20.25)	135 (15.92)	518 (17.44)	4598 (18.34)
Middle	809 (19.41)	407 (14.89)	611 (14.13)	357 (13.90)	245 (20.69)	248 (16.76)	663 (22.10)	405 (22.65)	95 (11.20)	548 (18.45)	4388 (17.51)
Matric	826 (19.82)	414 (15.15)	717 (16.58)	490 (19.07)	237 (2.02)	312 (21.08)	703 (23.43)	420 (23.49)	70 (8.25)	750 (25.59)	4949 (19.75)
Sr. Secondary (Intermediate)	67 (1.61)	33 (1.20)	56 (1.29)	38 (1.48)	35 (2.96)	27 (1.82)	54 (1.80)	29 (1.62)	14 (1.65)	62 (2.09)	415 (1.65)
Graduate	75 (1.80)	22 (0.80)	52 (1.20)	35 (1.36)	25 (2.11)	32 (2.16)	65 (2.17)	29 (1.62)	14 (1.65)	62 (2.09)	415 (1.65)
Post-Graduate	5 (0.12)	4 (0.15)	12 (0.28)	2 (0.08)	3 (0.25)	–	5 (90.16)	1 (0.05)	–	–	13 (0.05)
Others	2 (0.05)	–	1 (0.02)	1 (0.04)	3 (0.25)	–	5 (90.16)	1 (0.05)	–	–	13 (0.05)
Total	4167 (100.00)	2732 (100.00)	4325	2569 (100.00)	1184 (100.00)	1480 (100.00)	3000 (100.00)	1788 (100.00)	848 (100.00)	2970 (100.00)	25063 (100.00)

Table 5.27 : Elected Representatives : Occupation

Occupation	Bhiwani	Faridabad	Gurgaon	Jind	Mahendra-garh	Panipat	Rewari	Rohtak	Sirsa	Sonepat	Haryana
No Occupation	250 (6.00)	139 (5.09)	482 (11.14)	135 (5.25)	405 (34.21)	186 (12.51)	568 (19.12)	143 (8.00)	70 (8.25)	412 (13.87)	2790 (11.13)
Agriculture	3197 (76.72)	1789 (65.48)	2645 (61.16)	1583 (16.62)	525 (44.34)	756 (51.08)	1591 (53.03)	1112 (62.19)	537 (36.32)	1614 (54.34)	15349 (61.24)
Labour/ Wage Worker	626 (15.02)	721 (26.39)	982 (22.70)	784 (30.52)	177 (14.95)	451 (30.47)	724 (24.13)	469 (26.23)	220 (25.94)	850 (28.62)	6004 (23.95)
Self-Employed (including wearing, Crafts-men, carpentry, tailoring, barber, private school teacher, etc.	32 (0.77)	57 (2.09)	95 (2.20)	19 (0.74)	35 (2.96)	60 (4.05)	49 (1.63)	24 (1.34)	9 (1.06)	42 (1.41)	422 (1.68)
Business (petty shopkeepers, dairy, brick kiln, etc.)	61 (1.46)	24 (0.88)	101 (2.33)	46 (1.79)	42 (3.55)	16 (1.08)	55 (1.83)	39 (2.18)	11 (1.30)	47 (1.58)	442 (1.76)
Others (Mali, snake charmer, rickshaw pullers, NGO workers)	1 (0.02)	2 (0.07)	20 (0.46)	2 (0.08)	–	11 (0.74)	13 (0.43)	1 (0.05)	1 (0.12)	5 (0.17)	56 (0.22)
Total	4167 (100.00)	2732 (100.00)	4325 (100.00)	2569 (100.00)	1184 (100.00)	1480 (100.00)	3000 (100.00)	1788 (100.00)	848 (100.00)	2970 (100.00)	25063 (100.00)

NOTES

1. Lewis Oscar, *Village life in Northern India; Studies in a Delhi Village*, Vintage Books, A Division of Random House, New York, 1958.
2. Beals. R., Leadership in a Mysore Village in Richard L. Park and Irene Tunker (eds.), *Leadership and Political Institutions in India*, Princeton University Press, Princeton, 1959.
3. Orenstein. H, Leadership and Caste in a Mumbai Village in Richard L. Park and Irene Twiner (eds.), *Leadership and Political Institutions in India*, Princeton University Press, Princeton, 1959.
4. Mehta. S.R., *Emerging Pattern of Rural Leadership*, Wiley Eastern Pvt. Ltd., New Delhi, 1972.
5. Chaudhary D.S., *Emerging Rural Leadership in an Indian State*, Manthan Publications, Rohtak, 1981.
6. Singh Hargian, *Panchayati Raj Administration in Haryana*, Indira Publication, Gurgaon, 1985.
7. Prem Prashant, Suresh, Singh Charanjeev, *Popular Participation in Rural Development*, HIPA, Gurgaon, 1996.

6

PANCHAYATS AT WORK

A Case study of JRY

Reduction of poverty has been one of the major objectives of our planning process since Independence. A number of programmes have been launched to alleviate poverty amongst the weaker and deprived sections of the society. Inspite of these programmes and policies, the problem of poverty, unemployment and underemployment in the rural areas continues to be a major problem. The high incidence of poverty in rural India is directly related to prevalence of large scale unemployment and under-employment. Majority of the rural population is landless and sustains entirely on wage employment. The rural work force continues to suffer due to excessive seasonality of employment, lack of wage employment opportunities and low wage rates. Migration of labour, discrimination between wages paid to men and women, distressed child labour etc., are common features in rural areas.

Efforts to provide wage employment as a short run strategy for alleviation of rural poverty, therefore, has been a major component of development planning in India. The approach document of the Seventh Plan also realised the importance of creating employment to alleviate poverty in the country. It states "since poverty is the product of unemployment and economic growth is dependent on increase in production in all sectors, the employment has to be planned with the dual objective of removal of poverty and improving productive resources". Poverty alleviation programmes in operation seem to have been conceived, designed and implemented with a view to provide immediate and short-term relief to the poverty groups who have not benefited by the trickle down effects of growth.

The success of poverty alleviation programme depends on the extent to which asset and skill distribution is gradually shifted in favour of the poor. The tasks of such shift for sustained and rapid reduction of rural poverty are not easy without the poor gaining control over the rural institutions like the Panchayati Raj Institutions in their all effective manifestations. Anti-poverty programmes are likely to result in considerable leakages to the non-poor without the exercise of group pressure of the poor.

One of the major wage employment programmes in the rural areas being implemented by the Panchayats was the Jawahar Rozgar Yojana (JRY) now named as Jawahar Gram Samridhi Yojana (JGSY).

CASE STUDY OF JRY

The Jawahar Rozgar Yojana was one such programme for providing wage employment to the unemployed and under-employed rural poor. The Yojana was started in April 1989 by merging the on going National Rural Employment Programme (NREP) and Rural Landless Employment Programme (RLEP) into a single rural employment programme. The main objective of JRY was to generate additional gainful employment for the unemployed and underemployed persons both men and women in rural areas. The secondary objective of the Yojana was creation of durable community and social assets. In brief the Yojana was designed to arrest the seasonality of wage employment and contribute to improvement in quality of life by providing supplementary source of income through wage employment and by creating community and social assets.

Jawahar Rojgar Yojana (JRY) primarily targetted to benefit people living below the poverty line in rural areas. Preference was given to Scheduled Castes/Scheduled Tribes and freed bonded labourers. Under the Yojana at least 30 per cent of employment was to be provided to women and 22.5 per cent of funds were to be spent on individual beneficiary schemes for the direct benefit of SCs/STs. JRY being a centrally sponsored scheme, the expenditure was shared between the Centre and the States in the ratio of 80 : 20. Central assistance was provided to the States on the basis of proportion of rural poor in a State/UT to the total rural poor in the country.

The unique feature of the programme was that its implementation was to be done by the Panchayati Raj Institutions. The major share of funds were to be utilised at the village level by the Gram Panchayats. At the district level, the responsibility of co-ordination, guidance and monitoring was vested with the DRDA/Zila Parishad. 15 per cent of JRY funds were allocated to Block Panchayats. Funds under JRY was distributed among DRDA's/Zila Parishads, Intermediate Panchayats and Village Panchayats in a district in the ratio of 15:15:70. JRY was to be implemented in a truly decentralised fashion by the village Panchayats with active participation of people. The programme also aimed at empowering the village Panchayats and people. As in other States in Haryana also, the Panchayats were discharged with the responsibility of implementation of JRY.

Methodology

To study the actual implementation of JRY by the Panchayats and their role, 15 Gram Panchayats of Rohtak and Kalanaur Blocks in Rohtak district of the State were selected. The objective was to assess the capability and capacity of the Gram Panchayats to administer such poverty alleviation programmes. The survey was conducted before JRY was restructured as Jawahar Gram Samridhi Yojana (JGSY). A total sample of 75 beneficiaries of JRY and 75 elected representatives were selected for the study. The elected representatives consisted of 15 Sarpanches, 15 Up-Sarpanches and 45 members of the Gram Panchayat as indicated in Table 6.1. The beneficiaries were identified on the basis of records available with the Panchayats and selected on random basis. The representatives were elected in 1994-95 in the first elections held under the New Panchayati Raj System after the 73rd Amendment Act.

Data was collected with the help of structured interview schedule served on the respondents. Information regarding the socio-economic background of the representatives, their awareness about JRY, types of assets created and their level of satisfaction with various aspects of JRY were collected. For effective implementation of poverty alleviation schemes, the rural leadership can play a major role. Therefore it is very important to know the social background of the elected representatives who are discharged with the responsibility of implementing JRY.

Table 6.1 : Position/Profile of Elected Representatives

Attributes	*Category*	*Frequency*	*Percentage*
Position in Gram Panchayat	Sarpanch	15	20
	Up-Sarpanch	15	20
	Members of Gram Panchayat	45	60
Total		75	100

The Sarpanch occupies a place of importance in the rural local governance and particularly in the implementation of JRY.

Resource Allocation

The expenditure under JRY is shared between the Centre and the States on 80 : 20 basis. Under this sharing basis from 1989-90 to 1993-94, Haryana was allocated a total of Rs. 10383.84 lakhs. The central share being Rs. 8307.07 lakhs and that of the State Rs. 2067.77 lakhs. However, a total of Rs. 11091.96 lakhs was released, out of which the Centre's share was Rs. 8721.52 lakhs and the States' contribution was Rs. 2370.44 lakhs. A total of Rs. 10589.90 lakhs was utilised. In 1994-95, the total allocation was of Rs. 2389.61 lakhs. The Central share was Rs. 1911.69 lakhs and States' Rs. 477.92 lakhs. The released amount during the same year was Rs. 1792.13 lakhs. The Central share was Rs. 1433.70 lakhs and that of the States' Rs. 358.43 lakhs. During the year, the total resources available including unutilised balance and the released amount was Rs. 2259.98 lakhs, out of which Rs. 1173.29 lakhs were utilised. It targetted to create 33.29 lakh man-days but could achieve to create only 14.33 lakhs man-days.

Similarly, during the year 1997-98, the total allocation for JRY was Rs. 1711.53 lakhs, out of which, the Central share was Rs. 1369.22 and that of the States' Rs. 342.41. The released amount including the balance of the previous year which was

Rs. 2030.94 lakhs. The Centre's share was Rs. 1624.75 lakhs and that of the States' Rs. 406.19 lakhs. The total utilised amount was Rs. 1865.60. During the same year the target was to create 16.11 lakh man-days but the actual achievement was only 11.12 lakh man-days.

Implementation of JRY by the Panchayats has attracted the attention of various agencies. The programme has not been able to achieve the desired objectives and a number of loopholes have been pointed out. The role of Panchayats in the implementation of JRY is itself debatable. The focus of the study is on the capacity of Panchayats to handle such schemes under the present administrative structure available at the local level. It was felt that to understand the role of the Panchayats in the implementation of various schemes it would be appropriate to have a in-depth study of one scheme. For this implementation of JRY was taken as a case study.

One of the major complaints against JRY pertains to its beneficiaries. Rural leadership, as stated earlier, is centred in the upper castes. They manage to corner most of the benefits meant for the poor. This has been confirmed in a number of studies carried out by various researches. We tried to ascertain the real situation from a cross-section of elected representative.

Social Profile of the Respondents

Age, Sex and Caste

Table 6.2 gives the profile of the respondents in terms of their sex, age and caste. It is evident from the table that 44 per cent of the respondents were below the age of 40 years. 32 per cent were from the age group of 41-50 years while 14.67 per cent from the age group of 51-60 years, 9.33 per cent were from the older age group of 61 and above years. If we look at the overall age pattern of the sample size, 76 per cent of them are below the age of 50 years. This indicates a shift in the nature and pattern of rural leadership. The shift is from the traditional rural leadership of elders, which played an important role in rural Haryana to a much younger rural leadership.

Table 6.2 : Sex, Age and Caste of Respondents

Attributes	Category	Frequency	Percentage
Sex	Male	47	62.67
	Female	28	37.33
Age	21-30	11	14.67
	31-40	22	29.33
	41-50	24	32.00
	51-60	11	14.67
	61 and above	7	9.33
Caste	High Caste	47	62.67
	Backward Caste	13	17.33
	Scheduled Caste	15	20.00
Total		75	100.00

As the democratisation of rural society takes roots, the pattern of rural leadership is also undergoing a change. Reservation of seats in favour of Scheduled Castes, Backward Classes and women has also contributed to this shift in rural leadership. The table also reveals that 62.67 per cent of the respondents were males and 37.33 per cent were females. With 33 per cent reservation for women in the Panchayat their representation in these rural local institutions has increased substantially. As far as caste composition of the selected Panchayats is concerned 62.67 per cent of the respondents were from the upper castes, 17.33 per cent from backward castes and 20 per cent belonged to scheduled castes. The still dominant position of the upper castes in the Panchayats is clearly apparent.

Education and Occupation

As far as education of the respondents is concerned, 45.34 per cent of them did not have any schooling at all as revealed in Table 6.3. 9.33 per cent had studied upto primary school level, 21.33 per cent were Matric while 6.67 per cent had studied upto intermediate and 4 per cent were graduates.

Occupation confers a social status on an individual. It is evident that 58.02 per cent of the elected representatives are agriculturists and 12.34 per cent are self-employed. 18.52 per cent are casual/agricultural labourers and generally belong to the weaker sections of the society.

Table 6.3 : Education and Occupation of the Respondents

Attributes	Category	Frequency	Percentage
Education	No schooling	32	45.34
	Primary	7	9.33
	Middle	16	21.33
	Matric	12	16.00
	Intermediate	5	6.67
	Graduate and above	3	4.00
Occupation	No Occupation	2	2.47
	Agriculture	41	58.02
	Casual/Agr. Labour	15	18.52
	Business	7	8.64
	Self-employed	10	12.34
Total		75	100.00

Previous Training

As a part of the JRY programme, the elected representatives are to be imparted training so that they are acquainted with the programme and are able to discharge their responsibilities and functions properly.

Table 6.4 shows that only 30.67 per cent of the respondents were trained in procedures relating to JRY and its implementation. 69.33 per cent had no formal training. Most of them had heard about JRY in the meetings with the local level officials. Even the Sarpanches were not very clear about the financial procedures as regards to JRY funds. It is also evident that only 9.33 per cent of the respondents had a copy of the JRY manual and most of them were the Sarpanches. But even they had not really gone through the manual. The working of the elected representatives lacks effectiveness because they lack procedural and financial knowledge about JRY. They depend on the local level officials for any clarification, which need not always be correct. It was equally surprising that two of them had a manual in English and they could not even read it. Lack of administration and financial knowledge about the scheme only leads to its haphazard implementation and breeds corruption in the process.

Table 6.4 : Training Programme and JRY Manual

Questions	Yes	No	Total
Were you trained for implementation for JRY?	32 (30.67)	52 (69.33)	75 (100.00)
Do you have JRY Manual?	7 (9.33)	68 (90.67)	75 (100.00)

Note: Figures in parentheses are percentages.

Previous Experience

One of the problems with the Panchayat leaders is that they do not have the required experience to handle various functions entrusted to them. They are not even aware of their powers and functions. Table 6.5 reveals that 82.67 per cent of the respondents were elected for the first time and did not possess any earlier experience of working in Panchayats – 12 per cent of the respondents were second time, and 5.33 per cent had been elected for the third time. During the field survey it was revealed in the discussion that no formal training was given to the representatives regarding their powers and functions.

Table 6.5 : Previous Experience in Panchayati Raj

Question	Responses		
	Category	Frequency	Percentage
How many times you have been elected to the Gram Panchayat?	First time Second time Third time Fourth time	62 9 4 -	82.67 12.00 5.33 -
Total		75	100.00

Knowledge about JRY

The elected representatives play a major role in the implementation of JRY. But most of them have been elected for the first time and even after three years of their election, even though they are implementing JRY in their Gram Panchayats, they do not have adequate knowledge about it. Table 6.6 reveals that most of the respondents are not even aware of the objectives of JRY. 72 per cent of the respondents lack information about JRY and its objectives. 10.67 per cent are well informed while 17.33 per cent have some or partial knowledge about the scheme.

It is observed that illiteracy, poverty and lack of confidence on the part of the elected representatives is the main cause for low level of awareness. Nearly 46 per cent of the respondents have no formal schooling hence they find difficulty in reading and writing. They are unable to play any role in decision-making and, therefore, depend on others for advice. As a result of this they do not initiate any developmental activity.

Table 6.6 : Knowledge about JRY and its objectives

Category	Number	Percentage
To a large extent	8	10.67
To some extent	13	17.33
Not at all	54	72.00
DK/NR	-	-
Total	75	100.00

Peripheral Role of the Gram Sabha

As per JRY requirements all plans for development are required to be discussed at the Gram Panchayat meeting. While preparing plan, care has to be taken to safeguard the interests of the weaker sections in the village and priority is to be given to the works benefiting the SC/women and other weaker sections of the society. The Gram Sabha has to be apprised of the progress in implementation of the programme atleast twice a year. But does this happen in reality became the question of our enquiry. It is a known fact that in most of the villages, the Gram Sabha do not meet; the decisions are taken by the Sarpanch and the lower level officials and resolutions plans are passed even without any discussions in the Gram Sabha.

As apparent from Table 6.7 only 16 per cent of the respondents agreed that the action plan is discussed in the Gram Sabha meetings. While 46.67 per cent are of the view that they are not discussed. A high percentage of 37.33 per cent are not aware or have no opinion about it. Similarly only 30.67 per cent of the respondents agree that the action plan is discussed in the Gram Panchayat meetings. 34.67 per cent replied in negative, and the same percentage of the respondents are not aware or do not know about it. If this is the situation among the elected representatives then the question is do the other members of the Gram Sabha know anything about the action plan. The Panchayat representatives, it has been found out during informal discussions in the field, do not like to discuss the action plan or the funds received by the Panchayats either in the Gram Sabha or the Gram Panchayat. There is no transparency in the working of the elected representative. Secrecy is maintained as regards utilisation of funds.

Table 6.7 : Preparation and Discussion of Action Plans

Statement	Yes	No	DK/NR	Total
Whether action plans are....				
Discussed in the Gram Sabha?	12 (16)	35 (46.67)	28 (37.33)	75 (100.00)
Discussed in the Panchayat meetings?	23 (30.67)	26 (34.67)	26 (34.67)	75 (100.00)

Note : Figures in the parentheses are percentages.

Availability and Utilisation of Funds

One of the major problems with poverty alleviation programmes is the irregularity of flow of funds. It is a fact that most of the funds are released in the last quarter of the financial year and, therefore, not utilised properly. Without regular flow of funds no programme can be successful. We wanted to know from the elected representatives about the receipt of funds for JRY programmes, their utilisation and whether the muster roll for payment is maintained properly or not. While discussing this aspect the elected representatives were not very comfortable in answering to these questions. Most of them preferred not to reply or showed ignorance. There have been large scale allegations of maintenance of bogus muster rolls.

Table 6.8 : Availability and Utilisation of Funds

Questions	Yes	No	DK/NR	Total
Are JRY Funds received regularly?	8 (10.67)	5 (6.67)	62 (82.67)	75 (100.00)
Whether muster roll is maintained?	32 (42.67)	13 (17.33)	30 (40.00)	75 (100.00)
Do you think the muster roll maintained is bogus?	19 (25.33)	13 (17.33)	43 (57.33)	75 (100.00)

Note : Figures in the parentheses are percentages.

Table 6.8 reveals that only 10.67 per cent of the elected representatives of the sample Panchayats agreed that funds were received regularly by the Panchayats. Most of them (82.67 per cent) either did not reply or were ignorant about the availability, amount and time of release of JRY funds to Gram Panchayats. As regards, maintenance of muster roll only 42.67 per cent of the respondents agreed that a muster roll was maintained for all works executed while 17.33 per cent denied. 40.00 per cent were not even aware about the maintenance of muster roll. It is also evident that only 17.33 per cent denied that the muster roll maintained is bogus. On the other hand 25.33 per cent of the respondents were of the view that it was bogus and did not conform to the JRY guidelines. It was mostly the Sarpanch who was aware of JRY funds and the maintenance of muster roll. It was observed during the survey that the Sarpanch did not share this information with other members of the Panchayat. In the utilisation of funds and the maintenance of muster roll there appears to be a clear nexus between the Sarpanch, Panchayat Secretaries and the local level officials.

It was also found that the payment of wages was quite irregular. The wages were ordinarily paid after the completion of work and measurement book by the Junior Engineer. This process is delayed at times to put pressure on the Sarpanch for certain gratification. In some cases the Sarpanch paid advance money from his own resources to the labourers/workers for the works executed and later on reimbursed it. The wage rates are also not followed as per norms but no disparity in wages was noticed between male and female workers. The Sarpanch had very little knowledge about financial rules and procedures. Most of them during the survey agreed that financial procedures were very complicated and due to low level of education it was difficult to follow them.

Involvement of Contractors

Another important aspect that was highlighted during the study was the involvement of contractors in the execution of JRY works and the selection procedure for giving employment. According to JRY guidelines works are to be taken up by the

Gram Panchayats. As for the involvement of the contractors Table 6.9 shows that 30.67 per cent of the respondents agreed that contractors were involved in the execution of JRY works. However, 56 per cent denied the involvement of contractors in execution of JRY works. It has been observed that wherever contractors were involved it was only in labour and not in supply of material. Some of the labour contractors were visible at the Block offices where a deal is struck with the JE and the Sarpanch for labour contract. The Sarpanches try to justify this on the ground that workers work more efficiently if the work is given on contract. The contractors prefer to employ male workers because of their higher work capability and output in comparison to female workers.

Moreover, there is no system of registration for giving employment to the unemployed in the village. Instead the Sarpanch and his close associates select the workers arbitrarily. Where labour contract was given, it was left to the wishes of the contractor to select workers of his choice. It has also been observed that some of the labourers brought by the contractor were from outside the village. This is against the very objective of JRY as JRY is aimed at providing gainful employment to the residents of the village itself. Sometimes the Gram Panchayat allows a skilled labourer to bring unskilled labourers of his choice from outside the village. The effect of this process ensures that lesser number of women workers are employed. On the other hand, the women workers do not prefer to work in their own village because of a number of social constraints.

Table 6.9 : Involvement of Contractors in JRY Works

Questions	Responses			
	Yes	No	DK/NR	Total
Whether contractors were involved in the execution of JRY works?	23 (30.67)	42 (56.00)	10 (13.33)	75 (100.00)

Note : Figures in the parentheses are percentages.

Table 6.10 : Durability of Assets

Questions	Responses			
	Yes	No	DK/NR	Total
Is the quality of Assets created good and durable?	58 (77.33)	10 (13.33)	7 (9.33)	75 (100.00)
Are the assets created being maintained?	34 (45.33)	36 (48.00)	5 (6.67)	75 (100.00)

Durability of Assets

Creating community and social assets in rural areas is also one of the secondary objectives of the JRY. The asset created should be durable and well maintained. However, it was found that some of the assets created under JRY badly needed repairs as their maintenance was poor. Table 6.10 reveals that 77.33 per cent of the respondents were of the view that the assets created under JRY was of good quality and durable as well. The elected representatives were not prepared to agree that the assets were of bad quality. Only 13.33 per cent felt that the assets were of poor quality. At places it was observed that the bricks used in construction were of inferior quality and not baked well. The problem is with the maintenance of the assets created. There are no separate funds earmarked for the maintenance of the assets with the Gram Panchayat. Moreover, the elected representatives prefer to undertake the creation of new assets than repair the older ones. Table 6.10 also shows that 48 per cent of the respondents said that the assets created were not being maintained well. As the financial positions of many of the Panchayats is dismal, maintenance of assets has become a problem. It is felt that some funds should be sanctioned for the maintenance so that the assets can be taken care of. On their own very few Panchayats can maintain the assets without financial support. It was also observed that very few Panchayats used local material in works undertaken under JRY. The inspection was also not done properly and except the Sarpanch other members of the Panchayat were not aware of the inspection that took place.

Peoples' Cooperation

The representatives were asked about the extent of cooperation they receive from the residents of the village and the local level officials. Table 6.11 shows that the elected representatives receive more support from the residents of the village. 74.67 per cent of the representatives received co-operation and support in implementation of JRY. The difficulty appears to be from the side of the local level bureaucracy. 65.33 per cent of the respondents were critical of the role of the officials and said that they created more problems. Most of them were of the opinion that the officials were always trying to find loopholes rather than supporting and helping them to implement the schemes properly. The representatives also complained that the work procedures and rules were so complicated that they could not understand them properly. This enabled them to depend heavily on the knowledge of the local officials who were rarely helpful. This also became one of the reasons for corruption and nexus developed between them and the local officials, which affected the implementation of the JRY schemes as per the guidelines. Complaints of corruption and malpractice was very common. Some residents of the village surveyed felt that it had become more of a money making business than a programme of poverty alleviation to help the poorer sections of the society.

Table 6.11 : People's Co-operation in JRY

Questions	Responses		
	Yes	No	Total
Are you getting the required co-operation from the village residents in implementation of JRY	56 (74.67)	19 (25.33)	75 (100.00)
Are you getting required co-operation from the local level bureaucracy in implementation of JRY?	26 (34.67)	49 (65.33)	75 (100.00)

Note : Figures in parentheses are percentages.

PERCEPTION OF THE BENEFICIARIES

The JRY is targetted to benefit people living below the poverty line in rural areas. Preference is to be given to the Scheduled Castes, the Scheduled Tribes and freed bonded labourers. At least 30 per cent of employment is to be provided to women under the Yojana and 22.5 per cent funds have to be spent on individual beneficiary schemes for the direct benefit of SC's/ST's. As discussed earlier a sample size of 75 JRY beneficiaries were selected for the study. Their identification was not difficult as their names were entered in the register maintained by the Panchayat. Among the beneficiaries selection of 75 of them was on random basis. Most of the beneficiaries were from the Scheduled Castes and Backward Castes.

The objective was to have an indepth enquiry as to what extent the benefits have reached the intended target groups. JRY is supposed to provide employment upto 50-100 days in a year to at least one member of each family below the poverty line in the village. Due to lack of fund the Gram Panchayats are not able to create the required amount of work to provide adequate employment.

Table 6.12 : Employment Provided under the JRY

Attributes	Category	Frequency	Percentage
No. of days employed in JRY in the last one year.	Less than 15 days	20	26.67
	16-30 days	48	64.00
	31-60 days	07	9.33
	More than 2 months	-	-
No. of days employed during the last month.	Less than 7 days	32	42.57
	8-15 days	18	24.00
	16-21 days	11	14.67
	22 and more days	14	18.67
Total		75	100.00

As is evident from the Table 6.12, JRY has not been able to generate adequate employment in the villages. During the last one year before the survey was held only 64 per cent of the respondents worked between 16-30 days. Only 9 per cent of the respondents had worked for more than 31 days but less than sixty days and none of the respondents had worked for more than 60 days in a year. Similarly, during the last one month 42.57 per cent were employed under JRY for less than seven days. 24 per cent worked for less than 15 days and only 14 per cent had assured employment between 16-21 days. Due to irregularity in payment of wages and short duration of JRY works, workers preferred to take up private works than the works under JRY.

Consumption Pattern of JRY Beneficiaries

The beneficiaries of JRY belong to families below the poverty line. They do not have resources and assets of their own except a small house. JRY provides employment to only few people and that also for a short time, therefore, income received through wages is very meagre. The beneficiaries have no other source of income. It is important to know the consumption pattern of the beneficiaries.

Table 6.13 : Consumption Pattern of JRY Beneficiaries

Category	Frequency	Percentage
Household Consumption	49	65.33
Repayment of Debt	11	14.67
Buying Consumer durable	7	9.33
Buying Productive Assets	–	–
Savings	8	10.67
Total	75	100.00

Table 6.13, reveals the consumption pattern of the beneficiaries. 65.33 per cent spend their income earned from JRY works for household consumption while 14 per cent of the respondents used it for repayment of debts. 9 per cent spent for purchasing consumer durable and 10.67 per cent of the respondents could make some savings from JRY earnings. Those who saved it were the skilled workers and few women workers. No permanent increase in the income of the beneficiaries has been noticed. Neither have they been able to alleviate their poor conditions of living. It provides only temporary relief.

Awareness about JRY

Even though the scheme has been operational for almost a decade yet its awareness as a scheme remains confined to the

Sarpanch and the local level officials. The residents of the village have very little awareness about it and its objectives. Even though people have been the beneficiary of the scheme yet they are hardly aware of it as evident from Table 6.14. Only 2.67 per cent of the beneficiaries were aware of the scheme to a large extent and 13 per cent to some extent while 84 per cent were not at all aware of the scheme. The beneficiaries of JRY know that they have been provided some relief and help by the Government but under what scheme, they do not seem to be bothered to know. This is mainly because the Gram Panchayat representatives do not share information with the people of the village and the type of scheme that is being currently implemented. Instead those being employed under JRY are only told that they will be paid wages at the rate for certain works that they have to execute. Moreover it has been observed that most of the workers are ignorant and are concerned with their wages and not the schemes under which they are employed.

Table 6.14 : Awareness about JRY

Attributes	Frequency	Percentage
Awareness	2	2.67
To large extent	10	13.33
To some extent	63	84.00
Not at all	–	–
DK/NR		
Total	75	100.00

Selection of JRY Beneficiaries

It is the responsibility of the Gram Sabha to select the beneficiaries of a scheme. JRY beneficiaries are people from below the poverty line. The selection of the beneficiary has been found to be generally arbitrary and on the likes and dislikes of the Sarpanch. Sometimes, even the local level bureaucracy manipulates the selection of the beneficiaries. Village groupism especially due to elections plays a role in the selection of the beneficiaries. The Sarpanch tries to benefit the people of his group.

Table 6.15 : Selection of JRY Beneficiaries

Who selected the JRY Beneficiaries?	Frequency	Percentage
Gram Sabha	7	9.33
Gram Panchayat	17	22.67
Sarpanch	28	37.33
Labour Contractor	13	17.33
Block Officials	–	13.33
Skilled Labourer	10	–
Total	75	100.00

Table 6.15, shows that 37.33 per cent of the beneficiaries are of the opinion that the beneficiaries are selected at the discretion of the Sarpanch. 22.67 per cent say they are selected by the Gram Panchayat and 17 per cent are of the view that the labour contractor chooses the beneficiaries. The Gram Sabha appears to have a negligible role in selection of beneficiaries. Even the skilled labour at times has a role in selecting the beneficiaries. However the selection is shown to be done by the Gram Sabha.

Payment of Wages

The payment of wages at regular interval has been a problem. The workers have to run after the Sarpanch in order to get wages. The workers had to wait for many days to get their wages as the measurement of their work is not completed in time and this adds to resentment. The unskilled labourers generally prefer to get wages daily or on weekly basis as they have no other source of income. There are also complaints that the wages of the women workers had been collected by their husbands and the money did not reach the actual women worker. Table 6.16 shows the satisfaction level regarding payment of wages. The system of wage payment has been through cash only. Though foodgrains used to be given as part of wages in the early 1990's it has been discontinued now. The workers who had worked at that time and had received food-grains as part of the wages complained that the foodgrains supplied was of inferior quality and so they preferred cash payment as they could use it as per their requirements.

Table 6.16 : Payment of Wages

Question	Responses				
	To a large extent	To some extent	Not at all	DK/NR	Total
Are you satisfied with the payment of wages under JRY.	8 (10.67)	13 (17.33)	52 (69.33)	2 (2.67)	75

Note : Figures in parentheses are percentages.

Table 6.16, shows that nearly 70 per cent of the JRY beneficiaries are not satisfied with the payment of wages for work done under JRY. Only 10 per cent are satisfied to a large extent. The beneficiaries alleged that there are certain workers who are close to the Sarpanch or the members of the Panchayat and they are favoured in payment of wages and also in being hired for JRY work.

JAWAHAR GRAM SAMRIDHI YOJANA (JGSY)

The primary objective of JGSY is creation of demand driven community village infrastructure including durable assets at the village level with a view to enabling the rural poor to have more opportunities for sustained employment.

The programme is to be implemented entirely by the Gram Panchayat and the funds to the Gram Panchayats will be released directly by District Rural Development Agencies/Zila Parishads. The Gram Panchayat is the sole authority for preparation of Annual Action Plan and its implementation with the approval of the Gram Sabha. The Gram Sabha has been empowered for approval of schemes/works. The Gram Panchayats can execute works/schemes upto Rs. 50,000 without technical/administrative approval. 22.5 per cent of JGSY Funds are earmarked for individual beneficiary schemes for SC's/ST's. The Gram Panchayats can suitably relax 60:40 wage material ratio for building up demand driven rural infrastructure and social audit is to be done by the Gram Sabha. The village level Monitoring and Vigilance Committee will oversee and supervise the works/schemes to be undertaken.

The DRDA/ZP is responsible for overall guidance, co-ordination, supervision, monitoring and periodical reporting.

It is a centrally sponsored scheme on cost sharing basis between the Centre and the States in the ratio of 75:25 and all works that result in the creation of durable productive community assets can be taken up by the Gram Panchayat under JGSY as per the felt need of the area/people. To build the capacity and capability of the Panchayat functionaries, the State Government will be provided an amount of Rs. 10 lakh or one per cent of the annual allocation; whichever is less, to meet the training expenses of officials/non-officials involved in the implementation of JGSY provided that atleast 50 per cent of this must be spent on the training of non-officials.

The budgetary provisions under JGSY for the year 1999-2000 was Rs. 1689 crores out of which Rs. 1655 crores have been allocated to the States/UTs. As per the guidelines of JGSY now 100 per cent funds allocated to the States/UTs would be available to the Panchayats which comes to Rs. 1655 crores. As far as Haryana is concerned during 1999-2000 (upto October) out of a total allocation of Rs. 2751.79 lakh, the centre had released 1031.92 lakh and the State Government had released Rs. 343.94 lakh totalling to Rs. 1375.80 lakh being released under Jawahar Gram Samridhi Yojana.

As the empirical data suggests the performance of the Panchayats in the implementation of JRY has not been very encouraging. It is time that the institutional support through Panchayati Raj and Zila Parishad, people's participation, micro level planning and rigorous monitoring should be streamlined to make the programmes much more effective and meaningful.

The Wage Employment programmes have not made a significant dent in reducing unemployment mostly among unemployed. Various gaps in implementation of poverty amelioration programmes such as beneficiary selection, choice of schemes, distribution of resources, delay in sanctioning of funds, non-availability of quality assets are some of the problems with these programmes. But still anti-poverty programmes will have to be continued for a long time to help the poor who do not have any assets or have meagre assets. It is time to strengthen the Panchayats and to impart adequate and proper training to all the newly elected Panchayat representatives so that they know the powers and functions and also basics of administrative and financial procedures involved in the implementation of a programme.

Major Findings

The major findings and suggestions of the study are as follows :

1. Majority of the elected representatives of the Gram Panchayats are not even aware of their responsibilities, powers and functions. They lack basic leadership qualities. Both in terms of knowledge and skills their capacity and capability to manage rural development programmes is very poor.
2. Before launching a scheme, training of functionaries involved in it is a prerequisite. This has not been given any serious thought in case of JRY. Training programme must be organised for the elected representatives and officials. This will help in proper maintenance of record and accounts as well as in the effective implementation of the scheme.
3. People's participation is very essential for the success of any scheme. Timely and adequate publicity of various schemes at the village level must be provided to the residents of the village. In order to provide information to the villagers, notice should be put up in the Panchayat Ghar or some common gathering place in the village. Publicity of the schemes should also be done through *munadi* (declaration). As of today, people are not aware of the various rural development schemes to enable them to take advantage.
4. For implementation of any scheme the instruction manual is very important. However during the survey it was observed that only few JRY manuals were available with the Gram Panchayats, and that also in English thereby beyond the comprehension of most of the elected representatives. It is mandatory that the JRY manual in Hindi alongwith latest instructions should be

provided to the elected representatives for effective implementation of the scheme. Otherwise language becomes a barrier.

5. Gram Sabha and Gram Panchayat meetings must be held regularly. These should be held at the Panchayat Ghar (*Parais*) and not at Sarpanch's house as is the present practice. It has been observed that some members hesitate to go to the Sarpanch's house for a meeting. In the Gram Panchayat meetings full details of JRY projects and annual action plans should be provided to all the members of the Gram Panchayat. Women representatives in the meetings may be encouraged to take keen interest in matters relating to various Rural Development Programmes. The participation of the proxies of women representatives should be discouraged. To check the embezzlement of funds, the Gram Sabha should exercise effective supervision and control over Gram Panchayat.
6. It has been observed that corruption is prevalent on a large scale in the execution of JRY works. There is a need to check this tendency and plug the loop holes. In a bid to control corruption, bureaucratic barricades should be removed by replacing the prevailing arrangement by provisions of 73rd Amendment which places the Panchayats in a pre-eminent position *vis-a-vis* DRDA and other district and Block offices. The Panchayats should be given a free hand in the execution of various schemes. Efforts should be made to regulate the quality of the works executed by the Panchayats.
7. The socio-economic profile of the beneficiaries shows an interesting pattern, of the total respondents 61.33 per cent of the beneficiaries were Scheduled Castes while 18.67 per cent belonged to Backward Castes. A few of the beneficiaries were from the upper castes. In terms of education most of the beneficiaries were illiterates and had hardly been to school. Most of them were landless and did not possess any asset except a small house in a bad condition. On record about one-third of the beneficiaries are females whereas two-thirds are

males. More than 77 per cent of the JRY – 80 respondent beneficiaries had jointly income between Rs. 10,000-15,000. Some of them were much below Rs. 10,000.

8. The impact of JRY on the income and employment of the beneficiaries has not been substantial. Increase in the income of the beneficiaries has been nominal. Under the scheme 24 per cent of the respondents received less than Rs. 1000 as income and only 8 per cent received more than Rs. 3000 but less than Rs. 10,000. Of the total, 68 per cent of the respondents received between Rs. 1000 to 3000 as additional income due to JRY. Under the scheme, about 27 per cent were provided employment for less than 15 days, 64 per cent for 16-30 days while only 9 per cent were provided employment for more than one month. The income received is only marginal and did not show much impact on the livelihood of the beneficiaries.
9. At present, the Sarpanch generally spends the JRY funds according to his wishes. In most of the cases, the Sarpanch enjoys the support of a small coterie of the members which is enough to constitute the quorum of a meeting and resolutions are passed. It would be appropriate to device monitoring mechanisms to check the activities of the Sarpanch which are detrimental to the growth of Panchayats. Perhaps a provision of 'recall' in the Act may act as a deterrent and ensure that he/she carries out the functions as per laid down norms and procedures.
10. The wage rates mentioned in JRY manuals are quite low in comparison with the prevailing wage rates (Rs. 65 for skilled and Rs. 48 for unskilled against the prevailing market wage rates of Rs. 125 for skilled and Rs. 84 for unskilled). As a result, labour is not easily available for JRY works and this is partly responsible for preparing bogus muster roll. Hence, wage rates should be at par with the prevailing market wage rates.
11. Wages are not regularly paid to those who are employed in JRY works. The payment of wages is

withheld for two to three months which is in violation of JRY's guidelines stipulating that wages should be paid to the workers, weekly or fortnightly depending on the desire of the worker. JRY's guidelines with regard to the payment of wages should be strictly adhered to both in letter and spirit. Regular payment of wages will attract workers to the scheme.

12. While implementing JRY a overall sound criteria may be adopted to select the villages. Alongwith SC population, resource potential of the village and backwardness of the village should also be taken into consideration while allocating the funds to the villages under JRY. Selection of the villages under JRY is vitiated by political and other extraneous considerations. The criterion of backwardness is hardly followed in the selection of villages for assistance under JRY. Needless to add that the criterion of backwardness alone should be the basis for the selection of villages under JRY.
13. The State supervision and control of works undertaken by the Gram Panchayats is negative in character. The Gram Panchayats are generally allowed to make mistakes till mal-administration results in gross neglect of duty or abuse of powers. The administrative and technical staff at the Block level hardly play the role of a friend and adviser to the Gram Panchayats in providing timely guidance. A high degree of co-ordination and coherence between them is essential to make the scheme a success and ensure that the benefits are delivered in the most efficient manner.
14. It was also found that Sarpanches favour specific area within the village for development which leads to factionalism in the village. This problem may be solved to a large extent by preparing a list of works to be undertaken in the village on priority basis and then lottery system may be adopted for taking up some work. The Block officials, particularly JE should be associated with the drawing of priority list of the works.

15. The Gram Panchayats are spending JRY funds mostly on pavement of streets, lanes with the result that other works get neglected. There is hardly a Gram Panchayat which has spent money on works such as land development, irrigation, soil conservation, housing, sanitation and social forestry etc. Hence, Gram Panchayats should also undertake other works under JRY.
16. The ratio of 60:40 (60 for wage and 40 for material) is not very rational. Most of the Gram Panchayats are spending 60 per cent of the grants on the purchase of material and 40 per cent on the payment of wages. At present, the usual practice for the Gram Panchayats is to purchase material out of their own funds and make the payment of wages from JRY funds. But this is not possible in case of Gram Panchayats with insufficient finances. In order to maintain the prescribed ratio and also to avoid audit objections, the Gram Panchayats usually make fraudulent entries in the measurement books. The ratio of 60:40 should be revised so that the Panchayats can have some flexibility in taking up works.
17. Funds allocated to the Gram Panchayats are very meagre. Majority of Gram Panchayats surveyed do not have adequate finances. The amount of instalment under the scheme on the average do not exceed Rs. 2000-3000. With this little amount no major work specially under JRY can be undertaken. The problem is further aggravated in case of small villages and Gram Panchayats without any independent source of income. Therefore, instead of instalments JRY funds should be released once in lump sum. Moreover instead of launching new schemes every year the quantum of funds of the existing schemes should be increased. At the same time the Gram Panchayats should be allocated more funds and these should reach the Panchayats directly.
18. At present, a lot of time is taken in approving the plans. This leaves very little time for the executing agencies to implement the plans by the end of the financial year.

Furthermore, funds also are released at the fag end of the financial year. Therefore, the approval of the plan should be granted expeditiously so as to enable the Gram Panchayats to complete the works before the end of the financial year. The Gram Sabha should be the sole body for approving the plans.

19. There are at present various rural development programmes having very little funds. These programmes are being implemented without any co-ordination and coherence with partial impact. In order that these programmes make the desired impact, there should be sufficient co-ordination among all the rural development, poverty alleviation and employment generation programmes. Panchayat Samiti should plan a major role in co-ordination of poverty alleviation programmes.

In brief if may be said that generally the beneficiaries were from the target group and the level of awareness about the schemes was very poor both among the beneficiaries and the implementing agencies. No formal training was imparted to them nor efforts were made to educate the people about the scheme. JRY has not been successful in its present form in making any significant impact on the income and employment of the targetted group due to a number of reasons. To a large extent, beneficiaries were not satisfied with the benefits received under the scheme. Only a few community assets have been created in the rural areas. Much emphasis has been laid on the laying of streets with little emphasis on their maintenance. Corruption and political interference seems to mar the execution of the scheme.

The survey has exposed the weaknesses in the implementation of JRY scheme. The elected representatives have not being trained to implement JRY works. The flow of funds is irregular and the selection of beneficiaries is not proper. Women do not get their share in employment under JRY, the problem of contractors remains along with non-payment of wages. The use of local material is very less and the assets that have been created need repairs and no grants are available for maintenance. The Panchayats to a large extent lack both the capacity and capability to handle such tasks. Government of India has periodically tried to fine tune the scheme and performance of JRY is monitored regularly by the State and the Central Governments. Concurrent evaluation of JRY has also been done even then problems continue to exist at the field level in the implementation of JRY.

Apart from the problems, it was observed that under the JRY and other programmes, the generation of wage employment was getting overriding priority with the result that in the process of creating employment durable assets were created. It was felt that a stage had come when the development of village infrastructure needed to be taken up in a planned manner. This could best be done by the Gram Panchayats, who were closest to the ground realities, and who could effectively determine their local needs. Accordingly, Government of India has restructured Jawahar Rozgar Yojana. The new programme which came into effect from April 1, 1999 is dedicated entirely to the development of rural infrastructure at the village level and is being implemented by Gram Panchayats. The new restructured JRY is called Jawahar Gram Samridhi Yojana. The new programme overcomes some of the loopholes of JRY.

REFERENCES

Azizur Rahman Khan and Eddy Lee, *Poverty in Rural Asia*, Bangkok, ILO, 1984.

Baidyanath Misra, *Poverty, Unemployment and Rural Development*, New Delhi : Ashish Publishing House, 1991.

Government of India, Ministry of Rural Areas and Employment, *Annual Report – 1997-98:* New Delhi, 1998.

7

PANCHAYATI RAJ INSTITUTIONS
The Reforms they Must Undergo

The Panchayati Raj Institutions have now come to stay in India. It is no longer possible to ignore them or to abolish them. They constitute the third tier of authority and represent the basic form of democracy in the country. During the last 50 years many changes have been made in their organisation, structure and mode of functioning. To some these changes may appear confusing. But each time a change has been made, it has been for the better. So there is a hope that one day the PRIs will emerge with their full potentials on the Indian political scene.

As brought out in this study, the PRIs suffer from series of problems. They are not functioning the way they ought to. There is definite scope for improvement. But let us keep in view the fact that no institution in the world functions as it ought to. All need improvement in their functional behaviour. May be, the PRIs need it more than others. They are relatively new institutions and have yet to develop positive conventions and traditions. Every attempt should, therefore, be made to improve their working. To think that they should be abolished because they have failed is not a constructive way of looking at them. If this principle has to be applied to all sectors of our life, then nothing will be left; every thing would have to be abolished.

The changes that we need in the working of the PRIs are two fold. First, they have to be further strengthened as legal and Constitutional authorities. Second, the people who are involved in their working too need improvement in themselves. In fact the second proposition is more important. No matter how good is the legal framework of an institution, if the people who manage it are not good, it would never achieve its objectives.

India at present is passing through a very difficult cultural phase. The old values that distinguished Indian culture from the rest of the cultural realms of the world and which made India great have weakened; and the new values that go with democratic functioning are yet to be evolved and universally accepted. Our thinking is still very feudal; we try to be democratic but when self interests are jeopardized we fall back on the old feudal values.

Mahatma Gandhi is the latest edition of what is best in Indian culture. But we know that we have failed to adhere to Gandhian values. There is a crisis of character in the country; a crisis that pervades all walks of our life including the local self-governance system. There is, however, a simmering hope; more and more people are realising the flaw in our thinking and behaviour. Our old values of truth, non-violence, *sarvodaya, vasudhaiva kutumbakam* and love and compassion are being revived and the new values of equity, democratic decision-making and self-preservation with concern for others, are being incorporated in them. There is an upsurge of humanistic thinking in the midst of hedonistic behaviour.

There is thus a hope to improve our democratic institutions at the national, State and grassroots levels. PRIs have a very special role to play in a country like India. They are training grounds for future leaders who would run our democratic institutions. Let us, therefore, work together and try to strengthen the PRIs too so that even those who are poor have a part in the decision-making.

MAJOR PROBLEMS

Lack of Participation

Non-participation of the people in the Panchayati Raj Institutions despite half a century of experimentation must be a major concern of all those who would like Indian democracy to be strong. This may be because of apathy of the people borne out of ignorance and illiteracy or because of institutional drawbacks forcing people to be outside the system.

This report brings out clearly that despite such good measures like reservation of seats for the women and weaker sections of the society, people in general continue to be apathetic to PRIs. Yet at the same time, the report also brings out the fact the change is apparent. The pattern and structure of local leadership is changing fast. It is of course a hopeful sign but if the participation remains limited to elected representatives and the people in general do not evince any interest in PRIs, the roots of local democracy would remain week.

Bureaucratisation

One of the major reasons behind the inadequate participation of the people in Panchayati Raj affairs is the unhelpful and overriding role of local bureaucracy. Bureaucracy has been at the helm of affairs during the British era. After Independence too, it has been in a commanding position. Its tendency to rule, instead of support, the people continues unabated. Even if there are rules which prohibit them from interfering in the affairs of the Panchayats, they manage to frustrate their efforts by conniving with the elected representatives.

Most of those who are elected to run the PRIs are not very highly educated nor do they have previous background or training. Given the overall atmosphere in which they have to function, they tend to join hands with the bureaucrats at the local level to keep these institutions dormant.

Efforts have been made in the past in several States to curb the tendency of the bureaucracy to come in the way of efficient functioning of the PRIs. Some good results have been seen at the Zila Parishad level in some States but on the whole the situation has remained unchanged. The reasons are many. The bureaucratic structure is well integrated from top to bottom. It knows how to manipulate and get the work done. The elected bodies are novices, and many of those who get elected are easily lured by the bureaucracy to follow their diktat.

Pradhan Raj

As one surveys the villages, one finds people becoming very apathetic to PRIs and often hostile to the elected representatives. Panchayati Raj Institutions are derisively called Pradhan Raj Institutions. It is the Gram Pradhan (in Haryana, he is called Sarpanch) who rules, not the people. Earlier, it was the Mukhia appointed by the Government who ruled the village; now it is the Sarpanch elected by the people at times with just 25 per cent of total votes pooled who rules. He connives with the local bureaucracy and tends to misuse the funds.

The meetings of the Gram Sabha are rarely held. Not even Gram Panchayats meets regularly. But the proceedings of the meetings which were never held are recorded with signatures or thumb impressions of people. Who prepares these proceedings? It is the secretary of the village Panchayat.

Maldevelopment

The nature of the developmental activities carried out by the Panchayati Raj Institutions are often termed as mal-development. It happens because there is no planning at the grassroots level. Even at the district level, planning is a misnomer. It is nothing but a collection of projects proposed by various departments and whetted by higher level bureaucracy.

As apparent from the report, the resources allocated to the Panchayats are misused and even embezzled. This happens because of the insensitivity of the elected representatives towards their duties and the destructive role of the bureaucracy.

The role of the members of the Parliament and State Legislatures is also unhelpful. They tend to belittle the PRIs and often over-ride them through various means. The MP and MLA funds have very serious adverse implications for the PRIs. In fact the funds which ought to have gone to the PRIs has been diverted to MPs, MLCs, and MLA. The works carried out under the aegis of these funds are not in conformity with the priorities fixed by the PRIs. It is MPs, MLCs and MLAs who fix the priorities. Despite all checks and balances, people question the very rationale of this scheme and often they vehementaly question the basis on which these funds are spent. They appear to serve the MPs, MLCs and MLAs more than the people themselves.

Corruption

Corruption is the bane of Indian society today; the PRIs are no exception to it. It was hoped that people's own representatives will act more honestly than bureaucrats. The hopes have however been totally belied. The electoral process is so vitiated that only those who have money and muscle power can even think of contesting, what to say of winning elections. Despite all the rules regarding election expenses, money flows like water. Even in Gram Panchayat election, contestants spend thousands of rupees. For Zila Parishad and Panchayat Samiti, the amount rises to lakhs. Those who win election with money power, cannot be expected to be honest. They have recouped the amount they have spent, and have to collect more for the next election.

Even those who do not spend too much money in local level elections (specially in reserved constituencies) do not have service motive. They consider their positions as an opportunity to make money. Ofcourse, there are exceptions. Many of the elected representatives are honest and try to serve the people to the best of their ability. But the general trends are really disturbing.

Corruption has its roots in the general morality pervading the society. Morality is not something that can be taught in adolescence. Morality is learnt from early age from the environment in which a child is brought up. Primary school offers the ground for moral education. Gandhiji laid lot of emphasis on moral education at home and school. For him primary education meant moral education plus 3 R's.

If there is corruption in the society today it means that our homes and schools are not bringing up our children the way they should. So there is need for introspection and reorientation of our education system. In the short run we need appropriate training programmes for all the elected representatives of the PRIs to inculcate in them a sense of responsibility towards their electors and towards themselves. We think there is a need to revive Gandhian values in India in a big way. Gandhi is the only leader respected in India. People would follow him if the message is given through genuine persons and reliable channels.

HOW TO BRING PRIs BACK ON THE RAILS?

Another Bout of Constitutional Amendment

In order to strengthen the PRIs, there is need for a new Constitutional amendment. The 73rd Amendment gave too much power to the States to scuttle the real intentions of the Constitution. Powers are there on paper but not in reality. In fact, nothing has changed except the electoral process.

The subjects, which come in the purview of the PRIs should constitute the Local List in our Constitution. Thus there should be three lists, instead of two: Central List, State List and Local List. The subjects falling in the local list should be in exclusive domain of the PRIs. The Finance Commission at the Central or State level should divide the revenues between the State and the PRIs following certain formulae as it is done between the Centre and the State.

The local level bureaucracy should be under the control of the PRIs. In fact there is a need to rethink about the whole bureaucratic structure. It must be in tune with the new democratic governance.

Primacy to Gram Sabha

Gram Sabha is the only body where each and every voter can raise his voice. It is unfortunate that this body has been totally marginalised. It has no role to play in the present set-up of the PRIs. They have legal backing but the law can work only when people at the helm of affairs including those who oversee the PRIs so wish. Their revival should get top priority in any measure to reform the system.

So long as the Gram Sabhas remain dormant, PRIs cannot carry out their assigned responsibilities. In our view, Gram Sabha should wield the real power; everything should emanate from it. It should function as general body and nothing should be done without its formal approval. Since a Gram Panchayat may consist of several villages, each village should have its own Gram Sabha for decision-making. Whatever work is to be done should be first approved by the respective Gram Sabhas. It should then go to the Gram Panchayat for whetting, and prioritisation. Again the execution of the work should be done under the supervision and guidance of the Gram Sabha.

As stated earlier, the Gram Sabha should be treated as the general assembly and the Gram Panchayat as its executive body. All decisions taken by the Gram Panchayat must have the sanction of the Gram Sabha. Gram Sabha must be informed of anything done to meet any emergent situation without its sanction and approval.

Secure Funding

Adhocism in the provision of funds to Gram Panchayats is a major stumbling block in their smooth functioning. Often the funds come as late as March 15. They have to be utilised before the financial year ends on March 31. In such a situation either the funds remain unutilised or they are mal-utilised. It becomes quite handy for the unscrupulous Sarpanches and Panchayat secretaries. They join hands in the nefarious task of embezzling the money.

In our view, the Panchayats should be given Block grants within three months of the commencement of the new financial year. For financial stability and security, it should be possible for the State Government to give, let us say, a sum of Rs. 500 per voter to each Gram Panchayat within a period of ten years as special fund. A Panchayat of 1,000 voters would get Rs. 500,000. This should be in addition to the annual grant the Government makes for each Panchayat. Let the Panchayats keep this amount in Government securities/fixed deposits in banks They can draw the interest accruing from it but not the principal. Whenever there is delay in receipt of funds from the Government, the Panchayats can fall back on the interest and carry forward their work schedule. Any savings from the annual allocation should not go back to the State Government; it should go to the account of the Panchayat.

We feel that this idea is worth examining by the Central as well as State Governments. Let us examine how much money goes to Village Panchayats each year. If all this money were spent rightly and judiciously, every village in India would have got practically all physical facilities that rural India in 2000 AD deserves. It is a sad commentary on our development effort of the last 50+ years that we do not have even primary schools for our children with adequate facilities.

There could be several reasons for this sad state of affairs. One of them and perhaps a very important one is the misuse of the funds allotted for rural development.

ENSURING MEANINGFUL DEVELOPMENT

Master Planning

A prerequisite for speedy and orderly development is perspective planning. Unless we know what we want to achieve in both short and long run, and what are the resources at our disposal, we cannot make any headway. Unfortunately, the planning component has been missing from PRIs. The Planning Commission, Government of India, assisted the State Governments in setting up planning offices at the district level. Offices are there but the people who work in these offices are totally ignorant of the planning principles and practices.

At the Block and Gram Panchayat levels, planning has been totally ignored. Projects come from the Central or State Governments for implementation. The question of planning does not arise. We have now reached a stage in our development process where planning has to be initiated at all PRI levels. There has to be a plan for the district, each Block of district and each Gram Panchayat of the Block. In our view this exercise has to done under the guidance of people who are trained in planning. It should not be entrusted to generalist civil servants as it is done at present. The Constitutional amendment provides for the constitution of District Planning Committees (DPC) but in most of the districts these have not been constituted so far.

Each city in India has a Master Plan; all urban developments activities have to conform to the plan. The master plan is a legal document; those who violate are punishable. India is a land of villages. But no one has so far thought of having master plan for each village of India. In the USA, there is a master plan for each farm. The plan tells which land has to be used for what purpose, agriculture, forestry, grasses, fallow, etc., what tillage practices are to be adopted in which plot; which fertilizers are to be used and in what quantity; and what crops are to be grown and where. Each county, which is equivalent to district/block, also has a perspective master plan.

All development activities have to conform to the plan. There is no reason why we cannot do similar things in India. In seventies there was an euphoria for Block level planning. Then we switched over to district planning. Now we have no planning at the local level. The district plans prepared by the planning office of each district has practically no relevance. Government funds are often tied to certain sectoral projects and the funds given by the MPs, MLAs and MLCs are tied to nothing (including the plan).

Thus there is almost total anarchy in local area development. In this anarchic situation, the PRIs cannot be less anarchic. We suggest that each State of India should select one district as a pilot project for planned development. Each village, Block and the district itself should have a Master Plan prepared by those who have formal as well as practical training in planning. And all resources available to these districts should be utilised as per plan stipulation. We are confident that the results would surprise every one concerned with rural development.

At this stage let us caution the reader. We are not saying that all problems would be solved just by scientific planning. What we are suggesting is that among the several essentials that need to be done to improve the working of the PRIs, master planning is one.

Application of Information Technology

Modern information technology can aid not only the planning process but also removing much of the corruption that is stalling rural development. We would like to give examples of application of IT in rural development.

It is now possible to get satellite imageries of even villages showing the location, area, physical characteristics and land use of each field. It should be possible to plan the scientific land use of each Gram Panchayat area. It would also help in the re-development of villages.

The use of satellite imageries can make a revolutionary changes in district and Block level perspective planning. Application of GIS would tell the exact situation with regard to the development of roads, canals, drainage system, village settlements, towns, bridges, etc.

Application of modern information technology especially the GIS would be very helpful in curbing corrupt practices in rural development. Let us give one example. It is a common knowledge that funds are spent on many development activities without any physical achievement. A road may be repaired but only on paper. The contractor got his payment and those who gave the clearance for payment received their share. The same road may be repaired again after a couple of years for there will be practically no record of what was done earlier. Even otherwise, there would be many explanations for why it should be repaired again.

With the application of GIS, it would not be possible. It would be possible to know, which work was done when, at what cost, and by whom just by pressing button of the computer key board. As such records would be available for any number of years and for any activity, it will not be possible for the corrupt officials and elected representatives to fool the people and the system.

Classification of Villages

All villages of India should be classified into, let us say, five categories :

1. Developed
2. Developing
3. Underdeveloped

4. Backward
5. Primitive

Each type should be well defined using measurable criteria for the purpose. Classification should be done by specially trained persons; not the bureaucrats and clerks promoted as officers.

To make the classification an instrument of development, there should be provision for re-classification after five years or a decade. The criteria for classification may also be changed for with time concept level of development also tends to change in the minds of the people.

Village classification would serve two important purposes. First, it would help identify the areas and villages which need more investment; and second, it will help planners and development officers keep track of the trajectory of development of each Gram Panchayat and thus each Panchayat Samiti and Zila Parishad.

Recapturing Gandhi's Vision of PRIs

"Independence must begin at the bottom. Thus every village will be a republic of Panchayat having full powers. It follows, therefore, that every village has to be self-sustained and capable of managing its affairs even to the extent of defending itself against the whole world".

– Gandhiji, *Harijan,* 28 July, 1946.

BIBLIOGRAPHY

Arora, Ramesh, K., *People Centered Governance;* Essays in Honour of Prof. K. D. Trivedi, Aalekh Publishers, Jaipur, 2001.

Bajpai, Ashok, *Panchyati Raj in India : A New Thrust,* Sahitya Prakashan, Delhi, 1995.

Bajpai, Ashok and Verma, *Panchayati Raj in India, A New Thrust,* Sahitya Prakashan, Delhi, 1995, Vols. 2.

Biju, M. R., *Dynamics of New Panchyati Raj System; Reflections and Retrospects,* Manas Publishing, New Delhi, 1998.

Calmen, Laslie, *Towards Empowerment – Women and Movement Politics in India*, West View Press, Sanfrancisco, 1992.

Chowdhry, Prem, *The Veiled Women, Shifting Gender Equation in Rural Haryana*, 1880-1990, Oxford University Press, Delhi,1994.

Desai, Vasant, *Panchayati Raj : Power to the People*, Himalaya Publishing House, Bombay, 1990.

Dhaka, S. Rajvir, *Participatory Development and Capacity Building*, SDF, New Delhi,2000.

Dutta, Prabhat K., *The Second Generation Panchayats in India*, Calcutta Book House, Calcutta, 1993.

Gopalan, Sarla and Shiva Mira, (ed.), *National Profile of Women, Health and Development India*, WHO, 2000.

Hooja, Rakesh and P.C. Mathur (eds.), *District and Decentralised Planning*, Rawat Publications, Jaipur, 1993.

Kauchik, Sushila, *Women Panches in Position : A study of Panchayati Raj in Haryana*, Centre for Development Studies and Action, New Delhi, 1997.

Kaushik, Shushila, *A Panchayati Raj in Action : Challenges to Women's Role*, Friedrich Ebert Stiftung, New Delhi,1995.

Kaushik, Sushila, *Women and Panchayati Raj*, Har-Anand Publications, New Delhi, 1993.

Khanna, B.S., *Panchayati Raj in India : Rural Local Self Government*, Deep & Deep, Delhi, 1994.

Mandal, Amol, *Women in Panchayati Raj Institutions,* Kanishka Publishers, New Delhi, 2003.

Mathur, Kuldeep (ed.), *Development Policy and Administration*, Sage Publications, New Delhi, 1996.

Mishra, Sweta, *Democratic Decentralisation in India : Study in Retrospect and Prospect*, Mittal Publications, New Delhi 1994.

Mishra, S.N. and Singh, S.S., *Roads to Model Panchayati Raj: Review of Panchayati Raj Acts in the context of 73rd Constitutional Amendment Act*, New Delhi, Mittal,1993.

Mukarji, Nirmal, *People's Representatives and Bureaucracy: The Interface in Panchayati Raj*, Institute of Social Sciences, New Delhi, 1995.

Mukherjee, Amitava, (ed.), *Decentralisation of Panchayats in the Nineties*, Vikas, New Delhi, 1994.

Pai, Manoj, Malini Nambiar, E. (ed.), *The State of Panchayats: A Participatory Prespective*, Samskriti, New Delhi, 2001.

Palanithurai, G,. *People's Perception of Politics: An Indian Perspective*, Kanishka Publishers and Distributors, New Delhi, 1995.

Palanithurai, G., *Perception of Grassroots Democracy and Political Performance*, M.D. Publications, New Delhi, 1995.

Palanithurai, G., (ed.) *Dynamics of New Panchayati Raj System in India*, Concept, Vol. 1&2, New Delhi, 2002.

Palanithurai, G., (ed.), *Empowering People: Issues and Solutions*,: Kanishka Publishers and Distributors, New Delhi, 1997.

Prashant Prem, Suresh Misra and Charanjeev Singh, *Popular Participation in Rural Development – Emerging Dynamics of PRIs in Haryana*, HIPA, Gurgaon, 1997.

Rajiv Gandhi Foundation, "Revitalization of Panchayati Raj in India", RGF, New Delhi, 1997.

Santha, E.K., *Political Participation of Women in Panchayati Raj (Haryana, Kerala, and Tamil Nadu)*, Institute of Social Sciences, New Delhi, 1999.

Sharma, S.R., *Panchayati Raj and Education in India*, Mittal Publications, New Delhi, 1994.

Sharma, Sakuntala, *Grass-roots Politics and Panchayati Raj*, Deep and Deep, New Delhi, 1994.

Singh, S.S. and Suresh Mishra, *Legislative Framework of*

Panchayati Raj in India, IIPA, New Delhi 1993.

Singh, S.S., Suresh Mishra and Sanjay Pratap, *Legislative Status of Panchayati Raj in India*, IIPA, New Delhi, 1997.

Singh. D.R., *Panchayati Raj and Rural Organisations*, Chugh Publications, Allahabad, 1990.

Vasant, Desai, *Panchayati Raj, Power to the People*, Himalaya Publishing House, Bombay, 1990.

Verma, S.L., *Panchayati Raj, Gram Swaraj and Federal Polity*, Rawat, Jaipur, 1990.

Vyasulu, Vinod, *Panchayats Democracy and Development*, Rawat Publications, New Delhi, 2003.

Wadhwani, M. and S.N. Misra, *Dreams and Realities – Expectations from Panchayati Raj*, IIPA, New Delhi, 1997.

Articles

Abraham, Joseph, "A Framework for Financial Resource Planning of Panchayats and Local Bodies", *Yojana*, 40(2), February, 1996, P. 23-24, 42.

Bava, Noorjahan, "Enhancing Financial Autonomy of PRIs: Tasks Before State Finance Commission", *Kurukshetra*, Vol. XLIV, No. 7, April 1996, p. 15.

Bhatt, S.C., "Why this Delay in Setting up PRI's", *Kurukshetra*, 43(7), Apri, 1995, pp. 37-39, 97.

Datta, Prabhat, "Democratic Decentralization and Panchayati Raj in India: Perspective and Practices", *Administrative Change*, 22(1), July-December 1994.

Datta, Prabhat, "Vilage Self-government in Post-Colonial India", *Kurukshetra*, 43(7), April 1995.

Datta, Prabhat, "Political Empowerment of Rural Women in India", *Administrative Change*, Vol. XXIV, No. 2, January – June, 1997, pp. 128-147.

Dhaka, Rajvir S., "Panchayati Raj Institutions in Haryana – A Field Study", *Kurukshetra*, New Delhi, December, 2001.

Dhaka, Rajvir S., "Panchayati Raj Institutions: Goals and Realities", *ASTI Journal of Training and Development*, Vol. II, No. 1, January – June, 2001.

Dhawan, G., "Panchayati Raj Institutions: 73rd Amendment – Apprehensions and Comprehensions", *Kurukshetra*, New Delhi, 43(7), April. 1995.

Dhillon, D.S. and B.S. Hansra, "People's Participation in Rural

Development Programme", *Kurukshetra*, New Delhi, Vol. XLIII, NO. 4, Januray, 1995.

Dubey, A.K., "Panchayati Raj: The Constitutional Perspective", *Kurukshetra*, New Delhi, 43(7) Apr. 1995.

Gala Chetna, "Women in Panchayats", *Manushi*, NO. 65, July – August, 1997.

Gangrade, K.D., "Power to Powerless – Dawn of Participatory Democracy", *Kurukshetra*, 43(7), April 1995.

Hirway, Indira, "Panchayati Raj at Crossroads", *Economic and Political Weekly*, 24(29), 22 July 1989.

Hooja, Meenakshi and Rakesh Hooja, "Panchayati Raj in Rajasthan : Policy issues and Concerns" *Indian Journal of Public Administration*, Vol 44, No. 3, July – September, 1998.

Jain, L.C. "Panchayati Act : Clerical in Outlook", *Deccan Herald*, 1993.

Jain, S.P. "The Emerging Phase of Democratic Decentralization in India: Some Issues", *Kurukshetra*, 43(7), April, 1995.

Jain, S.P. "The Gram Sabha: Gateway to Grassroots Democracy", *Journal of Rural Development*, Vol 16, October – December, 1997.

Joshi, Uma, "Panchayati Raj Institutions: Grey Areas Galore – Need for time-bound tackling", *Kurukshetra*, Vol. XLVII, NO. 7, April, 1995.

Kirti Kumar, "Seventy-third Constitutional Amendment – A Reality for Women" *Journal of Constitutional and Parliamentary Studies*, 28(2), January – June, 1994.

Kotvi, M.S., "Empowerment of Women" Gender Equity – A Myth," *Jounal of Constitution and Parliamentary Studies,* The Institute of Constitutional and Parliamentary Studies, New Delhi, 1999.

Mathew, George, "Will Reservation Ensure Participation," *Social Welfare*, 42(5-6), August – September 1995.

Meenakshi Sundaram, S.S., "Empowerment of Women through Panchayati Raj", *Administrator*, 40(3), July – September, 1995.

Mishra, S.N. and Sweta Mishra, "Future of Panchayati Raj after 73rd Constitutional Amendment Act", *Kurukshetra*, Vol. XLII, NO. 7, April, 1995.

Mishra, S.N., "Decentralised Planning for Rural Development", *Kurukeshetra*, Vol. 48, No. 5, Feb 2000.

Mishra, Suresh and Rajvir S. Dhaka, "Institutional Mechanism for Participatory rural Development", *Kurukshetra*, June, 2001.

Mishra, Suresh and Rajvir S. Dhaka, "Role of Governance Institutions in Sustainable Human Development", *Kurukshetra*, June, 2001.

Mishra, Suresh & Dhaka, Rajvir, "Revitalising Panchayati Raj – Away from Gram Swaraj", in Anil Dutt (ed.), *Rediscovering Gandhi*, Mittal Publications, New Delhi, 2002.

Misra, Suresh, "Decentralisation, Development and Panchayati Raj," S.P. Nagendra. (ed.), *Development and Change Emerging Perspectives*, Concept Publishing, New Delhi, 1994.

Mitra, Amit, "Will Women in Panchayat Transform Bengal?" *Down to Earth,* July 15, 1993.

Mohanty, Bidyut, "Panchayati Raj 73rd Constitutional Amendment and Women", *Economic and Political Weekly,* 30(52), 30 December, 1995.

Mukherjee, Neela, "Rural Women and Panchayati Raj Institutions", *Kurukshetra*, June, 1994.

Narayana, K.S., "Karnataka Gram Panchayats – One year in Office Experiences from the Field", *Kurukshetra*, Vol. XLIII, No. 3, April, 1995.

Oommen, M.A., "Emerging Structure of PR in India" A Comparative Analysis of New Acts of States", *IJPA,* Vol. XL, No 4, October – December, 1994.

Panda, Snehlata, "Emerging Pattern of Leadership anong Rural Women in Orissa", *IJPA,* Vol. XLII, October – December, 1996.

Panda, Snehlata, "Women in Rural Local Government", *Kurukshetra,* 43(7) April, 1995.

Rajendran, T. and B. Kumauesan, "Panchayat in Raj and Rural Development 73rd Amendment", *Kurukshetra*, August, 1997.

Ramanujam, K.N., "The Philosophy of Rural Development", *Kurukshetra*, Vol. XLIII, No. 4, January, 1995.

Ramathilgam, G., "The 73rd Constitutional Amendment and its Implications for Women", *Kurukshetra*, 43(7), April, 1995.

Rangta, Rao, S.P., "Constitutional (73rd Amendment) Act: What Next" ?, *Kurukshetra,* 43(7), April 1995.

Reservation for Women in Panchayats, *Economic and Political Weekly*, 24(23), 10 January, 1989, pp. 1269-70.

Roy, M. Sam, "Emerging Panchayat Leadership and Polarizaton of Political Power at Grassroot Level", *Journal of Rural Development*, 14(4), October – December, 1995.

Santhananam, M.K., *50 Years of Indian Republic*, Publications Division, Ministry of Information and Broadcasting, Govt. of Indis, 2000.

Sanwal, Mukul, "Panchayat Raj Act: Without Substance", *Economic and Political Weekly,* 30(30), 29 July, 1995.

Sheth, Pravin, "Panchayati Raj for Development and Social Change", *Employment News,* Viol.. XIV, No. 16, Saturday, July 15, 1989.

Singh, Chandra B.P., "Panchayati Raj: Power to People", *Third Concept,* 9(97), Mar. 1995.

Singh, S.K., "73rd Constitutional Amendment: Analytical Frmaework", *Administrator*, Vol. XXXVIII, October – December, 1993.

Singh, S.K., "Panchayati Raj: Stumbling Blocks in its Path", *Kurukshetra*, Vol. XXXIV, No. 6, April, 1986.

Singh, Sitaram, "Revitalisaton of Panchayats", *Kurukshetra,* Vol. XXXIV, No. 6, April, 1986.

Singh, Surat, "Haryana New Panchayati Raj Legislation: A Critical Review", *Journal of Rural Development,* 14(1), January – March, 1995.

Singh, Surat, "Special Issue on Grassroots Democracy – Challenges Ahead: Second Anniversary of Constitution (73rd Amendment) Act," *Kurukshetra,* 43(7), April, 1995.

Srivastava, K.B. "State Panchayats Fiscal Relations: Issues before State Finance Commission", *Journal of Rural Development*, Vol. 14(3), pp.197-230,1995.

Suresh Misra, "New Trends in Community Initiatives: Panchayats in Action", *Journal of Rural Development,* Vol. 21(3), NIRD, Hyderabad, 2002.

Suri, P.C., "Panchayati Raj: Facts and Fiction", *Mainstream,*26(48), 10 September, 1998.

INDEX

Accountability, 17, 46
Action Plan, preparation and discussion, 140-41
Administrative system, 14
Age old pension, 45
Agricultural resources, 2
Agriculture Development Officer, 46
Allocation for Panchayats, 57
Andhra Pradesh Panchayat Raj Act, 1994, 79
Anganwadi centres, 18, 45
Annual Action Plan, 149
Anti-poverty programme, 150
Anti-social elements, 101
Ashok Mehta, 10
Ashok Mehta Report, 13
Assets, 3, 4
Assistant State Election Commission, role of, 91-92
Audit taxation, 54
Awareness about JRY, 146-47

Bahadurgarh, 53
Ballot papers, symbol, design and size, 87-88
Balwant Rai Mehta Committee, 10-11, 12, 28
    recommendations of, 11-13
    report, 70
Barwala, 53
Beals, R., 108
Bhaichara Panchayats, 26
Bhiwani, 119
Block level planning, 106
Block Panchayats, 12, 21, 28, 133
Bogus muster rolls, allegations of maintenance, 140-41
British Rule, 7, 26
Bureaucracy, 44, 50, 74, 161

Centrally sponsored schemes, 47, 56, 59, 152, 156
Changing electoral processes, 69-80
Chaudhary, D.S., 109
Chief Executive Officer (CEO), 39, 40, 41
Community development, 5
Community development annual plan 2001-2002, 59-61
Community Health Centre, 46
Consolidated funds, 15
Constitutional Amendment, bout of, 163-65
Contestants, qualification of, 77-78
    two-child norms, 78
Corruption, 13, 137, 144, 152, 162-63
Counting of votes, 88-89
Criminal activities, 101

Decentralisation, 12, 22
    scheme, 7
Declaration of results, 89-90
Democracy, 158
Democratic institution, 74
Democratisation, 71
Development activities, 166

Discrimination, 131
Distressed child labour, 131
District Election Officer (Panchayat), 81
District Planning Committee (DPC), 165
District Rural Development Agencies (DRDA), 47
Districtwise polling stations, 97
Drinking water supply, 59

Economic development, 3
Education system, 162
Elected representation,
  accountability of, 17
  education and occupation, 128-29, 136-37
Elections, 69
  conduct of, 81-82
  expenses of, 162
Election Commission, 21
  responsibility for conducting fair election, 69-70
Election petition, 90-91
Election rules, 80-82
Election symbols, allotment of, 85-86
Electoral wards, delimitation of, 83
Eleventh Finance Commission (EFC), 56
Embezzlement and wasteful expenditure, 52
Employment, 141, 144, 145, 153
Employment generation programme, 156
Ensuring meaningful development, 165-66
Environmental security, 1
Ernestine, H., 108
Executive Engineers Panchayati Raj, Hissar, 54

Faridabad, 119
Finance Commission, 21
Financial budget, 54
Financial management, 55
Financial resources, budget, account and audit, 50-51
First Phase election, 95
Free and fair election, 82
Funds, utilisation of, 140-41

GDP, 1, 3
Government, three tier system, 29
Government schemes, 4-5
Government of India resolution, 7
Gram fund, 50
Gram Panchayats, 11, 12, 15, 18-19, 21, 22, 27-28, 30, 75-77, 80-84, 87-90, 110, 133-35, 153-55, 161-65
  administration, 33
  age composition of, 112-13
  annual budged of, 37
  dissolution of, 35
  districtwise categorisation, 125
  duties of, 23
  educational status, 113-14
    occupational background, 114-15
  embazzelment/misappropriation of funds, 51
  financial and fiscal powers, 34-35
  funds allocation to, 155-56
  JRY funds to, 141-42
  number of wards reserved in, 106-107
  provision of funds to, 164
  ration cards preparation of, 45
  receipts and expenditure of, 33-34
  representative of weaker

section, 31
resolution or orders, 27
responsibilities, powers and functions, 151-52
sub-committees of, 33-34
trajectory of development, 168
Gram Pradhan, 18, 161
Gram Sabhas, 15, 17, 30-32, 163-64
funds utilisation of, 139-40
problems, 29
secure funding, 164-65
Gram Sabha Abhiyans, 18
Gram *Swaraj*, 4
Gram Vikas Nidhi, 48
Gram Vikas Samities, 48-50
Grassroots democracy, 13

Haryana falls in line, 21-24
Haryana, Panchayati raj system in, 28-30, 49-50
two-tier panchayati raj system, 28
Haryana Government, guidelines for works, 56-57
Haryana Municipal Corporation Act, 97
Haryana Panchayati Raj Act, 1994, 30, 74, 101, 102
Haryana Panchayati Raj Election Rules, 79-80
Haryana Panchayati Raj Rules, 76, 82, 83, 85, 87, 88

Illiteracy, 139, 159
Indira Gandhi, 14
Industrialisation, 2
Information technology, 166-67

Jammu & Kashmir, 11
Jawahar Rozgar Yojana (JRY), 132-35
annual action plan, 152
employment provides, 145
funds, 133, 137-38, 153-54
implementation of, 134-35, 138-39
perception of beneficiaries, 144-45
programmes, 137, 140
resource allocation, 134-35
schemes, implementation of, 144, 156-57
training programme, 138-39, 151-52
works, involvement of contractors in, 142-43
Jawahar Gram Samridhi Yojana (JGSY), 133, 149-50
Jind, panches and sarpanches, 44-45

Kurukshetra Panchayats, 47

Land reforms, 72
Lewis, Oskar, 108
Limits of election expenses, 98-99
Local audit department, annual report 1998-99, 52
Local autonomy, 10
Local Fund Audit directory, 59
Local level development projects, 5
Local self-government, 22, 159
Lord Mayo, 7
Lord Ripon, 7
resolution of, 8-9

Madhya Pradesh, 11
Mahendergarh, 119
Maharashtra, 11
Mahatma Gandhi, 4, 159, 162-63
Mandal Panchayats, 12
Mandi Dabwali, 53

Master planning, 165-66
Maru Singh Ad-hoc Committee, 78
Metcaffe, Sir Charles, 6
Migration of labour, 131
Misra, R.P., 24
Misutilization of funds, 55, 165
Model Code of Conduct, 86
Modern democracy, 7
Money power and alcohol use, 98
Montague-Chelmsford Report, 9
Moral education, 162
MPs, MLA, funds for, 166
Mukhia, 161
Munadi (declaration), 151
Muster roll, maintenance of, 140-41
  payments, 54

Nahar, 53
National Extension Service, 11
National Rural Employment Programme (NREP), 132
New Panchayati Raj System, 133
Nomination papers, scrutiny of, 84
  withdrawal of, 86
Nomination and scrutiny, 83-84

One man one vote, 69

Panches and Sarpanches, election of, 94-95
Panchayat annual plan, 2001-02, 60
Panchayats,
  announcing cash incentives of, 103
  audit of accounts, 51
  financial management, 55
  general elections, 94-95
  powers and functions of, 32-34
Panchayat representatives, two-child norm of, 78
Panchayat elections, 15, 20, 94-105, 110
  presiding officer's role, 93-94
  returning officer's role, 92-93
  unanimous elections, 102-103
Panchayat election/bye-elections, 98
Panchayati Raj, evolution of, 6
  previous expenditure, 138
Panchayati Raj Elections, 70-71, 73-74
Panchayati Raj Institutions (PRIs), 26, 28
  Gandhi's vision of, 168
Panchayat Samitis, 11, 28, 30, 35-37, 75-77, 80-83, 87-90, 162-64
  age classification, 123-24
  audited financial position of, 55
  chairman powers of, 36-37
  committees of, 38-39
  conduct of business, 38
  educational level, 124-25
  financial and fiscal powers, 38-39
  functions and duties, 37-38
  funds of, 38-39
  number of wards reserved, 106
  power and duties of, 40
  recommendations of, 46
  revenue and expenditure, 66
Panchayati Raj System, 6, 11, 44-46, 47
  failure of, 17-18
Panipat, 119
People's Cooperation, 143-44
People's participation, 23
Planning Commission, 50, 108, 165
Political accountability, 69
Political factionalism, 13
Political leadership, 21
Pollution, 2

Post-independent development, 27-29
Poverty allevation programmes, 131-33, 140, 156
Pradhan Raj, 161-62
Prashant, Prem, 109
Pre-independent development, 6-7
Primacy to Gram Sabha, 163-64
Pro-urban development policies, 2
Protection of Civil Rights Act, 1955, 77, 101
Public distribution system, 46
Punjab, 11
Punjab Gram Panchayat Act, 21, 27, 28
Punjab Gram Panchayat Samitis Act, 21
Punjab Village Panchayat Act, 26, 103
Punjab Zila Parishad Act, 21

Rajiv Gandhi, 14, 29
Rania, 53
Representatives of Peoples Act, 1995, 75
Resource allocation, 134-35
Restriction, 79
Returning Officer (Panchayat), 84, 92-93
Rewari, 129
Rohtak, 129
Royal Commission on decentralisation, 9
Rural areas, 2
Rural economy, 2
Rural development, 167
  annual plan, 59-62
Rural Landless Employment Programme (RLEP), 132
Rural leadership, 108, 135
  democratization of, 108
Rural politics, foundations of, 108
Rural and urban areas, civic services in, 59-60

Sanitation, 59
Sarkar Aapke Dwar, 44
Sarpanches, age composition, 117-18
  caste composition, 116
  education level of, 118
  election of, 87-88
  office terms of, 31-32
  powers of, 32-37
Sarvodaya, 159
Scheduled Castes and Scheduled Tribes (SCs & STs), 13, 112
  individual beneficiary schemes, 149-50
  preferences of, 145
  reservation of seats, 15, 21, 36, 79-80
Second phase election, 96
Secure funding, 164-65
Selection Committee of *Anganwadi* Workers, 45
Sixth Five Year Plan, 23
Sonepat, 119
State bureaucracy, 29
State Election Commission, 85-86, 110
  appointment of, 74-75
  direction and control of, 76
  free and fair panchayat elections, 105
  responsibility of conducting the election, 96
State Finance Commission, recommendations of, 58
Supreme Court of India, 114

Swaraj, 4
73rd Constitutional Amendment Act, 15-16, 21, 29, 48, 56, 108, 109, 119, 133

Taxation, 26, 27
Tenth Finance Commission, recommendation of, 56, 58-60
Three-tier Panchayati Raj System, 13, 21
Training programme, 162
Transfer of schemes, 59
Tubewell system, 47
Two-tier Panchayati Raj System, 28

Unanimous elections, 102-103
Unemployment, 131
Union Ministry of Rural Development, recommendations, 18-19
Unskilled labourers, 142
    payment of wages, 148-49
Up-Sarpanch (Vice-Sarpanch), 30, 50, 133
    office terms of, 31-32
Urban industrial development, 3
Use of vehicles, restriction on, 100-101
Uttar Pradesh, 11

Vasudhaiva Kutumbakam, 159
Videography of election, 99-100
Villages, classification of, 167-68
Village leadership, 108
Village Panchayats, 5, 9, 15, 21, 22, 46, 161
Violence in election, 104-105
Voters list, preparation of, 77, 80-81

Wage employment programmes, 180
Water supply scheme, 47
Weaker sections, reservation of seats, 79-80, 160
West Bengal, 11
Women, reservation of seats, 18, 36, 80-81, 115, 160

Year of the Gram Sabha, 19
    package of, 19-20
Younger rural leadership, 135

Zamindars, traditional leadership, 108
Zila Panchayat, 110
Zila Parishad, 11, 12, 15, 21, 22, 28, 30, 52, 75, 76-80, 83-88, 100-102, 162
    abolition of, 21, 28
    age classification, 123-24
    duties and functions of, 42-43
    educational level, 124
    funds, 42
    meetings, 41-42
    occupational level, 124
    revenue and expenditure, 67-68
    seats reservation for, 40